AF493344

unBROKEN

A study in Brokenness and Intimacy with God

Lois Massyn van Heerden

Lois Massyn van Heerden

COPYRIGHT

Copyright by Lois Massyn van Heerden – January 2022

The right of Lois Massyn van Heerden to be identified as the author of the work has been asserted in accordance with the Copyright Act 98 of 1978.

All rights reserved, whether the whole or part of the material is concerned, specifically the rights of translation, reuse of illustrations, recitation, broadcasting, reproduction in other ways, and storage in databanks. No part of this publication may be reproduced or transmitted in electronic, print, web, or other formats without the express written permission of the author.

Published by:

Lois Massyn van Heerden

Contact

Lois Massyn van Heerden
email: loisvanheerden@gmail.com

Edited by

Lois Massyn van Heerden

DTP

Clive Thompson
International Professional Book Designer
www.getclive.com
email: cliveleet1@gmail.com
cell: +27 83 761 0698

Contents

DEDICATION

... to my Creator ...

the One whom my soul loves

The Japanese art of Kintsugi Explained

In Japan, when a vase breaks, instead of throwing it away, it is repaired with gold that is literally inserted between the cracks to hold the pieces together. It is done because it is believed that a broken vase can become even more beautiful than it was originally.

But what matters is not so much the possibility of repairing an object by increasing its beauty and value, as the underlying philosophy, that maintains life, consists not only of integrity, but also of rupture and, as such, should be accepted.

The pain as well as the error, for the Japanese, does not embody a feeling to be eradicated or hidden, just as aesthetic imperfection is not an element capable of ruining the harmony of a figure; the cracks of the broken object must not be hidden or avoided but accepted and valued, just as the scars and wounds of the soul are not hidden but exhibited without embarrassment, being the same part of man and his history.

Kintsugi shows us that a form of beauty and superior perfection can be reborn from a restored wound, from the slow reparation resulting from a rupture, leaving us to understand that the signs impressed by life on our skin and in our mind have value and meaning, and that it is from them, from their acceptance, from their healing, that the processes of regeneration and inner rebirth that make us whole again in a new way.

Credit: Melissa Muldoon September 18, 2020

Photo Credit Cover: Studentessa Matta, Deposit Photo
www.artlovingitaly.com/the-japanese-art-of-kintsugi-explained/

Thanks and Acknowledgements

I would like to express my sincere gratitude to the following people whose input and counsel about this, my first book, I consider absolutely invaluable.

Werna Haupt

Werna Haupt, you have been my role model from the first time we met. You are the most-godly person I have ever had the privilege of knowing. The fragrance of Christ surrounds you and it is the sweetest thing to be in your company and experience Jesus in you. Thank you for taking the time to go through my manuscript a few times and testing the spirit and the accuracy of the content against the Word of God.

Thinus Byleveld

Thinus Byleveld, thank you for patiently reading my book (while I know you had 1000 other things to do!) I sincerely value your contributions, your thoughts, your experiences, the precious revelation that God gave to you during your journey. Thank you for the brutal honesty and transparency with which you shared your "from the dust" stories and your thoughts and interpretations of the things I shared. Thank you for being a soundboard for me!
Thinus Byleveld, Christian Entrepreneur and Counselor

Jesus Christ, my Lord and King

Lastly, to Jesus Christ, my Lord and King. Thank You for carrying me through all the years of testing and trials; thank You for allowing me to see You and to experience firsthand your unending grace and undeserved mercy ...

— · —

FOREWORD

I have known Lois van Heerden for 26 years. This book does not only reflect generic truths but also real-life experiences. Through this book, I witnessed the pieces of her shattered heart that were accumulated with immense courage to help others who might go through the same struggles in life. Lois does not only share her walk-through physical struggles, but also the deep emotional struggles that she had to face through her faith journey.

While being a member of the worship team under Lois's leadership for five years (1995 – 2000), I have experienced an intimacy with God that I never experienced again since – not even when I led a worship team myself. She has the worship heart of David – expressing her heart's longing after God through the songs that we sang, and by that she led people in the presence of God like the Great Shepherd himself would do. I remember the many people who received healing (physical and emotional) during the worship under the great measurement of grace on her calling. In fact, the anointing during the worship time with her was not experienced as "something" (like goosebumps), but as SOMEONE who showed up time and again during her powerful prophetic worship.

Furthermore, when I went through a divorce in 1996, her clear and distinct prophetic gift uplifted me in many ways when I was down and out and without direction. She, together with her husband, helped me stand up in my manhood and calling again without compromising one inch on Godly integrity. Lois gave direction and clarity of purpose in a time of emotional turmoil and uncertainty. I am convinced that she is stronger in her calling and gifting than many men of God due to the humility and brokenness that she carried alone all these years.

In 2005 (during the time that they lived with us in our house), I experienced Lois to be carrying the heart of Esther for the people of God.

Portraying such beauty and heavenly fragrance of God, I believe that she would have been chosen by the king as was Esther. In the same vein, I whole-heartedly believe that she has been chosen by her King, Christ Jesus, to pen down His heart for people (for whom He suffered and shed His blood) during times of immense brokenness.

Subsequently, I recommend this book to each and every person who is experiencing emotional and physical struggles. Not many children of God will stay focused in their faith-walk when they feel that God does not protect them emotionally and does not heal their bodies; however, that is exactly what Lois is living.

As Psalm 112 says:

> His (her) heart is steadfast, trusting in the Lord.
> His (her) heart is established;
> He (she) will not be afraid...

Thinus Byleveld
Christian Entrepreneur and Counselor

COMMENTS ON (UN)BROKEN

I was deeply touched and challenged by the contents of this manuscript. It stirred the passion in my heart for the presence, fellowship and intimacy with my Father, and a deeper desire to spend more time with Him. A new level of commitment, yieldedness, and commitment.

Lois, you speak from experience, walking through a crucible, the wilderness where God purifies, prepares, changes and shapes His children into the image of Christ.

My prayer is that Father God will use the depth of this word to give hope, new levels of faith, endurance and perseverance to the Bride of Christ, as we await the soon return of our Saviour, the Lord Jesus Christ.

Werna Haupt

PRELUDE PART 1

It was the 23rd of December 2014.

I was fit and healthy, and was in the Virgin Active gym in Hillcrest, power-walking on the treadmill. It was two days before Christmas and there was much that I wanted to do.

Out of the blue, I became very dizzy.

Taking a good gulp of water, I tried to ignore the dizziness and kept on walking. After a while I realized, I was going to faint and made my way to the reception desk, holding on to apparatus and training equipment as I walked. I quickly explained to the young girl at the desk that I feel like I'm going to pass out and, believing it was my blood sugar that had dropped, I asked her if they could maybe get me a Powerade or Coke .... anything with a lot of sugar.

I went to the ladies' changing rooms feeling extremely light-headed and lay down on one of the wooden benches. After a few minutes, a handsome young trainer walked into the ladies' room with a cold drink in his hand and asked how I felt. Obviously, he had some emergency medical training and wanted to determine whether this was serious or not. I persuaded him that it was probably just my blood sugar that had dropped and that I would be fine after the cold drink.

I sat up slowly and drank the Powerade not feeling well at all. In addition to the dizziness, my chest was now feeling constricted and it felt like my head was going to explode from pressure. I sat down a few more minutes, the trainer coming to check on me every now and then. I realized I couldn't stay there and had to get home.

Feeling very funny, dizzy, short of breath and slightly disorientated, I reached the car and drove home.

I spent the rest of the day mostly laying on the bed, trying to shake off the dizziness, nausea, the tightness in my chest an overwhelming feeling of fear and anxiety.

Early evening, I took a sleeping pill and other medication, yet, I battled to sleep and woke up the next morning still feeling much like the day before.

It was the day before Christmas. Tomorrow was my birthday when I would turn 57. None of our children would be there as it was the in-laws' turn to have them there.

I had a leg of lamb to cook and other preparations to make, to give my husband and me some feeling of celebration. I was still very dizzy and it felt like the blood was pounding in my head. I was very short of breath and extremely anxious.

Being believers in Jesus Christ and the fact that He purchased health and healing for all His children on the cross, my husband prayed for me and somehow, I got through the day.

Prelude Part 2

Christmas morning dawned with shades of bright gold and rosy pink streaking the eastern horizon.

Many of us have gone through fiery trials and tests of our faith. For some, it may have been a debilitating illness. For others, it might have been the indescribable pain of the loss of someone they loved. Even others might have experienced the numbing ache of failure upon failure, rejection, the destruction of a marriage that has fallen apart or a business that has gone bankrupt.

Whatever it may have been, there is no doubt that God tests and tries His children whom He loves dearly. It is with utmost certainty that I can say that if you are a laid-down lover of God, who seeks Him wholeheartedly, and lives a life completely surrendered to Him, you will at some point, be "hammered into pieces," thrown into the crucible and put into the searing heat of the fire.

Malachi 3:3 says that "He will sit as a refiner and purifier of silver; He will purify the Levites and refine them like gold and silver; ..."

This process continues until the Refiner is satisfied with the quality of the silver which has come forth from the fire. Only when He can see His own image reflected clearly in the molten silver will He take the silver out of the fire.

Although this process is almost always accompanied by much pain, grief, sorrow and despair, there is also a different test that God uses to test the faith and mould the character of one who loves Him. This test can prove even more difficult to go through than the former.

The name of this test is called, "The Test of Success." Not even the test of being in the fire of God can reveal the heart of man like the Test of Success.

Nothing brings to light the true character of man and exposes the hidden motives and personal agendas the way success does. Give a man (or a woman!), power, money, fame or success, and you will clearly see what he/she is made of!

It is one of the most difficult things for a child of God to learn to bring both the most scathing criticism, and the most flattering praise and accolades to God; to kneel before Him to ask for healing from the painful words from another, or on the other hand, to lay down the praise and admiration and adulations of man as an offering to Him.

The Bible confirms this in Proverbs 27:21 where it says, "The crucible is for silver and the furnace for gold, and a man is tested by the praise accorded to him."

Praise and adoration of man are dangerously addictive! Our carnal man seeks constantly to please man and win the approval of man, or to be in favour with the rich and influential who might open the right doors for us!

What is the test that lies before you today and how will you fare in that test?

Whatever it may be, may God give us grace to cling to Him for life and death; may we be constantly aware of the fact that we need Him desperately, even for our next breath. May we come out of the crucible shining and only reflecting the image of the One Who has waited patiently for us to be perfected in His hand!

— · —

PRELUDE PART 3

The next month passed mostly in a blur. I would feel extremely anxious for no apparent reason, take one of my wonder-pills and spend the rest of the day on the bed. When I arose from my drug-induced sleep, the cycle would simply repeat itself. I found myself in the grip of unrelenting, totally irrational fear and was struggling to cope with normal, everyday chores like cooking or doing the washing.

Panic attacks would often just overcome me, and I would find myself, clawing at the sheets of the bed in absolute terror, struggling to breathe, my heart beating completely out of control and the blood pounding in my head. During this time, my husband rushed me to the hospital a couple of times, as I displayed all the symptoms of a heart attack. I was at the doctor's almost every week, searching for answers to what was happening to me.

A few days into January 2015 it was as if I received an epiphany of what had actually triggered this crisis in my body. It dawned on me that I had, in a moment of utter insanity, just stopped taking an anti-depressant that I had been on for 15-plus years.

Years before, I was diagnosed with Myalgic Encephalomyelitis (ME), more commonly known as Chronic Fatigue Syndrome or "Yuppie Flu." Although many people who are diagnosed with this illness are not affected by it to such an extreme, I was hit by it to the point of being almost debilitated. Apart from the severe, blinding headaches, a constantly aching body and extreme fatigue, my sleeping pattern was completely disrupted. I was unable to sleep.

In our search for a solution, my doctor and I started to experiment with different medications and combinations of medication and eventually found that a certain anti-depressant worked very well, as it prevented and helped relieve the migraines, and also helped me to sleep. Thus, I was put on an anti-depressant. As the years progressed my dosage gradually increased until I was taking quite a high dose every day.

Those who are acquainted with the side effects of anti-depressants will know that one of them is weight gain. For years I had been struggling to lose weight in vain. I worked hard in the gym and ate healthily, but never lost an ounce. As I searched for answers, I realized that it was the anti-depressant I was taking that prevented me from losing weight.

And thus it happened, that on one sweltering hot day in December 2014, I decided I am not going to take those tablets ever again. It was 10 days later that I found myself in the emergency room of Hillcrest Hospital.

Slowly I started connecting the dots as I read about the withdrawal symptoms of antidepressants.

Horrified I realized that I had made a very big mistake by simply stopping to take the pills cold turkey. My health and my life were flung into a downward spiral from which I was unable to escape.

I decided to visit my GP and told him what had happened and my self-diagnosis of the challenges I experienced. He assured me that the withdrawal symptoms could only last for two or three weeks so it could not be that, but nevertheless, he put me back on the anti-depressant, albeit, a lower dosage this time, as well as a new tranquillizer.

Feeling hopeful, I returned home with my new batch of pills.

In the months and years to come my health continued to deteriorate like an aeroplane dropping out of the sky. Ironically, I started losing weight at a frightening rate. Within a matter of weeks, I literally became skin and bone. Every organ in my body was affected. My hair fell out and my teeth deteriorated markedly. I began to experience sensory issues and could not bear the feeling of my clothes against my skin. At night the sheets would 'hurt' me. I literally had to force-feed myself to get at least a little nourishment. I could not stand the taste of milk, because "I could taste the cow!" One of my favourite things to eat is a lamb chop. To my shock (and my husband's!) I couldn't bear the taste, because I could taste and smell the sheep!

My hearing became overly sensitive and I would freak out at any sounds or noise that, for others, seemed quite normal. Going to a restaurant was a nightmare as I struggled to follow a conversation with all the noise in the background.

Around February 2015, I started to experience excruciating pain in my lower abdomen, lower back, and legs. Going to the doctor, again and again, her diagnosis fluctuated from being allergic to gluten to having too many toxins in my body, to having me admitted for depression in a hospital where I would have to do cleaning, cooking, washing etc. I can't remember how many times I 'detoxed' but think that after two months or so, I was relatively toxin-free!

In a fit of frustration, I lost my temper with her one day and told her "if she ever mentions one word again about allergies or wrong diet I would not ever come back!"

At the lowest point of my weight loss, I was in so much pain, I would often cry myself to sleep only to wake up two hours later, screaming in agony. White-hot pain seared through my back, my hips and my legs constantly.

Emotionally I was flung into a never-ending vortex of depression, suicidal thoughts and anxiety. I was unable to cope with the normal and mundane things to be done in a household. I remember bursting into tears one day when I had to make a sandwich for our garden help! I couldn't bear the sound of my grandchildren (whom I absolutely adore!) screeching and laughter as they played around the house. Quietly I would retreat to my bedroom where I would shut the door, close the curtains and curl up in my bed.

Once I decided to go to a nearby shopping mall, 'just to get out of the house.' Within a few minutes, I was so exhausted I couldn't walk anymore. Deciding to go home, I realized that I couldn't remember where I had parked the car. Struggling to remember I became more terrified by the minute. Eventually, I had to check every parking lot to find my car.

My life had become a grey haze of pain, brain fog and confusion. I would struggle through the days, almost unable to wait until it became 17:00 or 18:00 so I could just drink a handful of pills and get some relief from the pain for a short period of time. I lost so much of my mobility from the lack of movement that I had become almost bedridden.

Eight months later a huge tumour was found at the back of my womb, pressing on my spine, and I was rushed to surgery. Thankfully it was benign. I was full of hope that all my pain had actually been caused by this tumour and would now be gone.

I was wrong.

Even as I was recovering from surgery, I felt the old familiar pain returning to my back and legs. Back to the doctors, again and again, I was finally diagnosed with severe spinal stenosis and spondylolisthesis – the cause of the pain! Strangely, I felt almost elated at finally knowing what was wrong with me. I had a name for this demon that was destroying my life! It was Friday and I was scheduled for surgery first thing Monday morning. Scared but hopeful I went home, only to receive a call informing me that my Medical Aid would not approve the surgery.

I was shattered. I wrote one appeal after the other but all were rejected on the basis of some totally insignificant technicality.

It would take three long years before my surgery would finally be approved.

It was during those three years that I encountered the risen Christ in the furnace of affliction. It was in the white-hot oven of searing pain that I discovered that I was not alone. It was there that I met the Son of God, face to face. It was there in the Refiner's fire that I learned that I, a mere mortal, can walk with a divine Creator every moment of every day.

And it was there that the writings in this book were born.

May you be blessed and healed as you read the pages of unBROKEN, and above all, may you be inspired and motivated to pursue a walk with God that is beyond anything that you could ever imagine!

> When you cross the threshold of the discipline of spending time with God because you have to, and step into the realm of spending time with Him because you cannot live without Him, you step into life beyond the veil. A life of uninterrupted intimacy, passionate desire, indescribable ecstasy, fulfilment that defies description. A life from which you will never want to turn back and never again be without!

Chapter 1

A Grain of Wheat falling into the Ground

Dying to self is the hardest thing you'll ever have to do. It is a laying down of your rights and refusing your flesh an opportunity to express a desire. It is a continual denial of every want, craving or demand of your flesh. It comprises a refusal of the right to be heard; a denial of the right to be treated fairly; an abdicating of your winning an argument or even the right to argue your point.

Dying to self implies exactly what it says – death. Death to self, death to selfish ambition, death to being acknowledged or understood.

In this process of dying, the biggest miracle of all takes place within you. The Seed of Life within you starts to germinate and new life is birthed. A life pure and holy; a life free from corruption. A heart washed from selfish motivation and cleansed from deceit. A life that needs no recognition or acclamation from man; a life that is not destroyed by injustice or unfair criticism because it has nothing to prove. Complete fulfilment and joy are found in simply glorifying its Creator.

Dying to oneself and refusing your fleshly desires and rights might be seen by some as weakness, but in reality, it is the same strength Christ displayed when He "was silent as a sheep before its shearers and opened not His mouth to defend Himself" while it was within His power to destroy His accusers. It requires much more strength to deny your flesh than to use the power of persuasive words and strong arguments to beat and humiliate those who contend with you!

Every time you choose to allow the carnal man to have his way you stint the growth of the Christ-life within you. Yet every time you refuse to respond in the flesh the divine nature within you blossoms and grows and the fragrance of Christ becomes stronger!

"Unless a grain of wheat falls into the earth and dies it remains by itself alone. But if it dies it produces many others yields a rich harvest" John 12:24.

From Conversations with God ...

Chapter 2

Refined as Silver

Many of us have gone through fiery trials and tests of our faith. For some, it may have been a debilitating illness. For others, it might have been the indescribable pain of the loss of someone they loved. Even others might have experienced the numbing ache of failure upon failure, rejection, the destruction of a marriage that has fallen apart or a business that has gone bankrupt.

Whatever it may have been, there is no doubt that God tests and tries His children whom He loves dearly. It is with utmost certainty that I can say that if you are a laid-down lover of God, who seeks Him wholeheartedly, and lives a life completely surrendered to Him, you will at some point, be "hammered into pieces," thrown into the crucible and put into the searing heat of the fire.

Malachi 3:3 says that "He will sit as a refiner and purifier of silver; He will purify the Levites and refine them like gold and silver; ..."

This process continues until the Refiner is satisfied with the quality of the silver which has come forth from the fire. Only when He can see His own image reflected clearly in the molten silver will He take the silver out of the fire.

Although this process is almost always accompanied by much pain, grief, sorrow and despair, there is also a different test that God uses to test the faith and mould the character of one who loves Him. This test can prove even more difficult to go through than the former.

The name of this test is called, "The Test of Success." Not even the test of being in the fire of God can reveal the heart of man like the Test of Success.

Nothing brings to light the true character of man and exposes the hidden motives and personal agendas the way success does. Give a man (or a woman!), power, money, fame or success, and you will clearly see what he/she is made of!

It is one of the most difficult things for a child of God to learn to bring both the most scathing criticism, and the most flattering praise and accolades to God; to kneel before Him to ask for healing from the painful words from another, or on the other hand, to lay down the praise and admiration and adulations of man as an offering to Him.

The Bible confirms this in Proverbs 27:21 where it says, "The crucible is for silver and the furnace for gold, and a man is tested by the praise accorded to him."

Praise and adoration of man are dangerously addictive! Our carnal man seeks constantly to please man and win the approval of man, or to be in favour with the rich and influential who might open the right doors for us!

What is the test that lies before you today and how will you fare in that test?

Whatever it may be, may God give us grace to cling to Him for life and death; may we be constantly aware of the fact that we need Him desperately, even for our next breath. May we come out of the crucible shining and only reflecting the image of the One Who has waited patiently for us to be perfected in His hand!

CHAPTER 3

THE PURPOSE OF THE FURNACE

The Fiery Furnace was designed by God to mould you; to change you... for the better.

- Don't flee from it
- Don't deny it
- Don't avoid it
- Don't attempt to get out of it
- Don't fear it
- Don't try to shorten the trial

Embrace it. Allow it to run its full course. Participate and yield to its working within you.

When He has purified you, you will come forth as gold. Touched and formed by the Master's hand. Moulded again and again you will become a vessel of honour, displaying the glory of the Potter. Useful and used in the hand of the skilled Archer you will be a polished arrow, hitting the mark every time. Melted and shaped in the heat of the furnace you will become one with the Artist Who is transforming you. You will take on His nature, His heart, His passion.

Embrace the furnace! Rejoice in the scorching heat of the flames, for the glorious thing about the furnace is that you're never alone when you're in it. It is there in the midst of the fire where you will see the glory of the Son of God.

The miracle of belonging to Him is not that you never go through the fire, but that when you go through the fire and the flames it has no power over you. You come through on the other side whole; not even your hair singed by a flame... not even a hint of the smell of smoke clinging to you. Forever changed by the indescribable grace and mercy of a loving God.

"When you pass through the waters I will be with you, and through the rivers they will not overwhelm you. When you walk through the fire you will not be burned or scorched, nor will the flame kindle upon you."

CHAPTER 4

YIELDEDNESS

A state of being where I am so wholly surrendered to the One I love that there is simply no refusal, no denying, no hesitancy to obey, no "no God," but only a "Yes Lord" left in me.

> Yieldedness is the focused desire to please my Lord and my King. No command is too hard to carry out; no unction too difficult to follow; no prompting too hard to obey. Like a woman smitten with her lover, it is just impossible to say "no."

Where initially it starts out as a deliberate choice to yield, the reward of His joy and His delight at your response quickly becomes an emotional fix and a spiritual high I simply cannot live without! It becomes the life-blood of my being!

This is the key that unlocks His presence; this is the door to the Secret Place where we can only sit wide-eyed and mystified in speechless wonder, marvelling at His indescribable beauty.

A yielded heart! This is the secret of a deep and intimate walk with Him! Where every trace of rebellion against His plan simply disappears; where every grievance against His will vanishes. Every sacrifice becomes a total joy! Every instruction a delight to follow. His every wish my greatest desire!

There is no place for anything but joyful compliance to every request and a heart at rest in His sovereign guidance.

"I take joy in doing Your will, my God, for Your instructions are written on my heart." Psalm 40:8 (NLT)

If the fear of God in your life is not greater than your desire to sin, you will never be able to live a life of total victory over sin. The fear of God protects you against temptation and the lusts of your flesh. Lois van Heerden

CHAPTER 5

NOTES ON DYING

It is in death that life is found. It is in dying that new life is born. It is in the laying down of the old and the corruptible that the putting on and the clothing with the incorruptible, eternal takes place.

It is in the white-hot heat of the melting pot where silver is refined and in the scorching flames of a fire where the purest gold comes forth – totally transparent without a fleck of dust or dirt.

It is when the delicate petals of a rose are painfully crushed underfoot or squeezed and broken when the sweet fragrance is released.

An exquisite pearl of great beauty is formed in a small, enclosed space, with constant, relentless irritation day and night. Multi-faceted and multi-layered diamonds of immense value and indescribable beauty are found in the depths of the earth. Unappealing, undesirable, unwanted as a charred, black chunk of coal, they lay hidden and unseen hundreds of metres beneath the surface. Under immense pressure, an object of indefinable beauty painfully slowly begins to take shape.

This is the story of sons and daughters of the Kingdom. The heir of the Father who will inherit everything. The son in the house. It is not the story of the bondservant who is bound by law to serve his master until the day he dies. The story of a son is much different from the story of a slave. The Lord disciplines those whom He loves; His own. He does not discipline those who are not His own.

Herein lies the key: Not in being dragged kicking and screaming to the mouth of a gaping oyster to be imprisoned for God knows how long! Not in being forcefully stuck into the soil hundreds of metres beneath the surface to spend years and decades under incomprehensible pressure in total isolation! No!

The key lies in total and complete surrender to the King of your heart. The key lies in yieldedness. The key lies in trusting, joyous abandonment to the will and ways of the Master. To allow Him to pick you up time after time and throw you once again on the Potter's wheel. Until you come forth ... a vessel of honour; a vessel of joy and absolute purity. A vessel totally rid and cleansed of even the tiniest speck of impurity or dross, but one who is the purest reflection of the One who created it.

CHAPTER 6

ABOUT STRUGGLING

Struggling is the catalyst for growth and change. When there's no struggle the status quo remains the same or declines. No change, no growth, no reformation takes place without a revolution against the current status quo.

It's only in the face of difficulty, challenge and hardship that our mind is changed, paradigms are shifted and we are forced to think differently. Struggling stretches us beyond set parameters and urges us to take roads unknown and make new discoveries within ourselves and our circumstances.

When the struggle is severe, it teaches us 'bendability'... flexibility... fluidity... the ability to flow with a force against which you are powerless. It works in us a willingness to surrender to the power of a raging river; allowing hardship to purify and refine you.

Sometimes one can be broken in the pain of struggle. For a child of God though, breaking is not the end, but often the beginning. Breaking is the beginning of beauty and glory forming within me as the sweetness of Christ grows within me and starts to seep through the cracks of a broken vessel.

Being broken is not something to fear or to resist but to the contrary, something to embrace and rejoice over. When one is broken, the Bible says that God is "near to us."

When the battle is fierce and the struggle becomes too much to bear... rest in the hands of the Master Potter – the One Who is close to you.

"The Lord is close to those who are of a broken heart and saves such as are crushed with sorrow ..." Psalm 34:18

Chapter 7

Trust

Trust is all about knowing the One Whom you are following. It does not matter at all where the destination is that He is taking you to, or how difficult the journey is to get there. It doesn't matter how strong or how high the walls of that fortified city are that He is taking you to, in fact, it is not even important that you know where He is leading you to.

That city may be named Life or Death; Sickness or Health; Poverty or Prosperity – it is not important. Even if the road He is leading you on is rocky, mountainous, dangerous or slippery, it matters not. All that matters is that I know the One Who is taking me there and leading me through it.

Because I know Him; I experienced His love; I have seen His faithfulness and tasted His goodness, my heart is still and my mind is at rest. Because I am with Him every road becomes a journey of discovery of another level of His grace; another dimension of His love.

To know Him is the core around which my entire life revolves and every circumstance or road life may take me on simply pales in comparison to the joy and wonder of walking with Him – My Father, my Friend, the lover of my soul!

"In You O Lord, do I put my trust and confidently take refuge; ..." Psalm 71:1

Chapter 8

Surrender

The key to more power; the 'secret' to greater anointing; the ingredient that gives you greater accuracy in the prophetic, more detail in the Word of Knowledge.

That thing that gives you more boldness when flowing in the gifts of the Spirit; that key to hearing God's voice clearly and accurately...

That key lies not in trying harder.

It is not found in more 'works' for God.

It is not found in praying more, praying longer hours, or reading the Bible more. (Although these are certainly wonderful and important!)

It is most certainly not in "strategizing" better, planning better and marketing more effectively.

This key is locked up and found in more surrender. Surrendering to God is the single most important factor in obtaining what all ministers of the gospel desire, namely, power to work miracles and great anointing. In what seems like an absolute oxymoron, the more you let go of your desire for these things, the more He gives it to you.

The more you lay down your dreams, your vision, your passions, the more He raises it up. As your desires birthed in selfishness and corruption are crucified and laid on the altar, godly dreams and desires birthed in the heart of God spring to life.

Complete surrender to God is something that is achieved by very few individuals. Without exception it is found in those who have gone through the crucible of fierce trials and tribulation; those who have been tested by the very fire of God.

The willingness to surrender to God and embrace and welcome every trial is the only component in our search for 'more of God', which can work a brokenness within you, and nothing touches God's heart more, than a broken spirit.

A heart that is so aware of its own failings and shortcomings and unworthiness, and at the same time totally overcome by the truth and reality of its stature in Christ.

Herein lies the secret: A heart that draws near to Him; a heart that seeks after God. A heart that has reached the place where power, name, fame, reputation, doesn't matter at all anymore.

Complete joy, utter fulfilment and satisfaction is found purely in God and He becomes your Delight!

CHAPTER 9

THE CRUSHING OF THE OLIVE

In the waiting on God, there is a crushing that takes place.

As with olives that are pressed and pressed and pressed again in order to collect the choicest, purest of the precious oil, and to capture the most of the rich smell of the olive.

The last pressing is done from what has become a sort of an olive paste which contains the flesh of the olive as well as the olive pips. This pressing produces the least oil of course, yet it captures most of the heart of the olive fruit; the delicious taste, the greenish colour so typical of the finest oils in the world.

So, it is in the waiting process.

Already you have lain down yourself so many times; already you have chosen to deny yourself and reckon yourself as dead over and over.

Yet, under the extreme pressure of the olive press, 'flesh and bone' is crushed to a pulp, and the purest oil of the fruit is released. Once again, a demonstration that in dying, life is birthed; in the process of being crushed, the purest form of life-giving nutrients of hope and healing are released from the prison of death, to bring joy and delight to everyone who tastes it!

> "But we have this precious treasure in unworthy, earthen vessels of human frailty so that the grandeur and surpassing greatness of the power will be shown to be from God [His sufficiency] and not from ourselves." 2 Corinthians 4:7

CHAPTER 10

WAITING

There is something profoundly powerful about mastering the ability to wait.

Waiting is one of the most difficult things to do for believers and unbelievers alike. It is a crucible of its own!

Waiting for a breakthrough, waiting for God's intervention in a difficult situation, waiting for the right time, waiting for the right partner...

Waiting, waiting, waiting.

Yet, locked up in the process of waiting, is a latent, life-changing force, able to bring forth change, like few other things are able to!

Waiting changes your character; it works patience in you that brings about growth and maturity that cannot be achieved in any other way. It teaches you contentment in having to accept and embrace something which is beyond your power to change.

Waiting works a meekness within you, a gentle embracing of the trial of your faith; an acceptance of the testing of the single-minded purpose that you are striving for. It brings about a willing surrender to a trial designed to test your commitment and unwavering steadfastness in staying the course to which He has directed your footsteps.

In the waiting, your heart is changed and your mind renewed. A mind-shift takes place and a deeper understanding of God and His ways and of life, in general, takes place.

Learning to wait, even when it seems like God has forgotten you, is a critical part of your journey as a believer.

When this deeper understanding comes, it releases a peace in your soul which surpasses all understanding. In fact, a peace that is greater than having no understanding at all!

Embracing the waiting changes your life completely. It brings unhurried ease to your steps; a restfulness and undisturbedness that is deeply satisfying. It sets you free from always chasing the goal! It delivers you from being a driven individual who has to achieve success within a certain period of time, to calmly accepting that every moment and every circumstance in your life has been known by your Creator from long before the foundations of the earth.

Waiting out an impossible situation finally brings you to that place where the realization truly sinks in:

He is in control!

With a good attitude and a soft, pliable heart, the difficult place of waiting, becomes the most beautiful, serene place, filled by indescribable peace!

> "But if we hope for what we do not see, we wait for it with patience." Romans 8:25

Chapter 11

The Place of Impossibility

It is often when you are at the lowest point in your life when God calls you to do something great. At that point where it is totally impossible in the natural – when you do not have the strength physically; you are drained emotionally – you do not have the finances or resources. That is often the moment God chooses to call you to do something for Him.

That place and that point of total weakness, total improbability and complete impossibility is God's time to choose and to send you!

That point where you are totally UNable is the point where God is able! That place where it is completely impossible is where God can demonstrate that anything IS possible!

It is very often in our biggest crises and our darkest hour that our greatest successes are conceived.

God chooses our moment of complete "impossibility" to birth in us a dream or a vision or calls us to do something that is so big that it is completely impossible for us to do.

That moment when you are at your lowest point; at your weakest; in the darkest place where you can't see the faintest glimmer of light or hope. When you've lost everything that provided you with some security or stability to lean on, and you have nothing left to give.

That is often the moment God chooses to speak to your heart a dream ... a calling that He wants you to fulfil ... that you are completely unable to do.

As with Abraham and Sarah, God waited 'till they reached "the place of impossibility" and then He said, "next year you will have a son."

Like Moses who had fallen from being a prince in a palace to shepherding sheep in the desert – for a Midianite priest. It was there in the desert that he received the word of the Lord to lead 2 million stubborn, stiff-necked Jews to a country as yet unknown to them.

Joseph had been forgotten about in prison and probably had no hope of ever getting out, let alone see his dreams fulfilled.

The "place of impossibility" becomes the womb where greatness is conceived. It is the most fruitful soil for visions, dreams and hopes to germinate and suddenly burst into life.

If you are there today, know that it is a good place to be. There where you have nothing to offer, nothing to give. Where all natural strengths, security and crutches have fallen away and it's just you in your complete weakness.

In this brokenness your heart is tender and yielded to God; your ear is inclined to hear His voice. You are ready to hear the Word of the Lord!

Speak Lord, Your servant is listening.

CHAPTER 12

THE STORY OF A VINE

A vineyard is the only fruit that fares best when under stress and duress.

Unlike other fruits that flourish in good soil and enough water, the vineyard produces its choicest fruit when it has been under extreme stress and hardship. The harvest of grapes is smaller, yes, but oh, the quality is superior!

Some of the best wines in the world are produced from vineyards that are planted in dry, rocky areas and the 'least favourable' soil. As a matter of fact, some vinedressers will deliberately give too little water to the vine, forcing it to send its roots deeper into the soil in an effort to find water.

The stressed vineyard will produce the most excellent grapes, in contradiction to its fellow vines, which may be planted close to a river in the fruitful soil. While the vine which has had more than enough water and no stress at all, produces bigger and more fruits, the quality of the fruit cannot be compared to the quality of the fruit produced by a vineyard that endured much stress.

The fruit which was grown and cultivated under difficult circumstances is so much sweeter than the watery taste of the fruit that was grown under perfect circumstances. The vineyard which had to push through dry, hard, rocky soil for some moisture and nutrients, and bears the merciless heat of the sun day by day, produces the sweetest fruit. Pruned relentlessly by the vinedresser, it captures within its very essence the distinctive aromas and richness of the vineyard where it is planted.

As it is with the vine, so it is also with us. The Vinedresser, the owner of the vineyard, loves His vineyard and checks continuously on the growth and welfare of the vine.

In actual fact, He even cuts away clusters of fruit that bear too little or too poor a quality, in order for the other fruit to produce better fruit. In pruning season, the vine is cut back ruthlessly, leaving it to appear dead and lifeless. A piece of wood, unable to ever bring forth fruit again. Yet, after this season, which leaves the vine weeping, the new season comes and quietly awakens the vineyard again. With a burst of life and energy new buds spring forth and push out new green shoots and soon little berries begin to form in clusters on the branches.

With unending love and patience, the Vinedresser tends and keeps His vineyard till the branches bend over with the weight of the sweetest, choicest fruit. A fruit that bears the unmistakable touch of the Master Vinedresser and is immediately recognized as cultivated and grown under His own hand.

"At least there is hope for a tree: If it is cut down, it will sprout again, and its new shoots will not fail. Its roots may grow old in the ground and its stump die in the soil, yet at the scent of water it will bud and put forth shoots like a plant." Job 14:7-9

CHAPTER 13

BARRENNESS

"Sing! O Barren One!"

I've been pondering on the well-known scripture in Isaiah 54:1 for a couple of days: "You who did not bear; break forth into singing and cry aloud, you who did not travail with child! For the children of the desolate one will be more than the children of the married wife, says the Lord."

What an astonishing thing to say to a barren woman! A woman who longs for a child of her own but she cannot have children! Yet, God says to her: "Sing! Praise Me!"

Then after He instructs her to sing, He gives her a promise: "The children of the desolate one will be more than the married wife." So, God first instructs her to praise Him and be joyful, and then He gives her a promise of children.

The promise followed the praise!

There is something profoundly powerful about praising God for something He promised even before that promise has been fulfilled. Praise 'unlocks' the promise! Praise makes the promise come alive! Praise 'gives flesh and bone' to the promise of God, and pulls it from the heavenly realm to manifest here on earth. When you start praising Him for something that has not happened yet, it is conceived in your womb.

Praise from the lips of a barren one moves the heart of God like nothing else! If you are barren and desolate; no fruit of your labour; unproductive, no harvest, no health, no finances ... Let your cry of praise pierce the heart of God this very day! Praising Him nourishes the 'promised child' you are carrying in your womb! Soon your time will come; the promise He has given you will become flesh and blood and will be born unto you!

Chapter 14

A Promise of God

A Promise of God

I was born in Namibia and grew up in Windhoek. My father loved fishing and we would often get in the car and drive to Hentiesbaai, one of the several small, fishing villages along the West Coast of Southern Africa. The trip would take us through the beautiful Namib Desert.

Most of the time when we drove through the desert, there was just nothing. Dry, desert sand, baking in the hot sun with a "tolbos" playing in the wind.

Sometimes, however, on our return trip home, we would be greeted with the most wonderful surprise – the desert would be covered in flowers! Vibrant and colourful flowers had sprung up everywhere! A small shower of rain had fallen and overnight thousands of seeds had germinated and pushed upwards through the soil to stand in colourful glory, their faces turned towards the sun!

A promise of God is like a tiny seed, which has locked up within its DNA, the ability to explode into life at the exact moment when the circumstances are perfect. These tiny seeds can lie dormant in dry, barren soil for years and years, and then one day, the waters of life reach into its heart and awakens it to life.

Many of us have promises that have been lying dormant in our hearts for years and years... and the cry of our hearts has often been: "When O God?!"

I believe we are in a season of rain; rain in the desert; rain of awakening promises; rains of the Holy Spirit bringing to life those promises we have carried within us for years or even decades!

Lift up your hearts and stretch out your hands to God and dance in the rain; drink in the rain!

The Holy Spirit says: "It's time!"

"For the Lord will comfort Zion, He will comfort all her waste places; He will make her wilderness like Eden, and her desert like the garden of the Lord; ..." Isaiah 51:3

CHAPTER 15

WHEN GOD SAYS "NO"

How do we react when we ask God for something and He says "No?"

All too often Christians recount stories of how we prayed and prayed for something and believed and stood in faith and made the right confessions and fought in the spirit, yet God "didn't answer our prayers." I myself am guilty of this.

As parents, it just seems like a natural thing to sometimes say "no" to our children. We do it all the time! No one questions our decisions and no one thinks that we don't love our children because we sometimes say "no." No! As a matter of fact, we will probably be applauded by the saying, "Well, a child can't always have his way."

Do we ever consider the possibility that sometimes when we ask God for something He could say "No?" And, why is it that when God doesn't 'answer our prayers' we are suddenly in a crisis with our relationship with Him? Why do we immediately make the assumption that He doesn't love me, His blessing is not upon me, He has withdrawn His hand from my life?

Can we as children of God, who are born from Him, who carry His DNA, the ones who call Him "Abba," accept the fact that He sometimes says "No" to our requests – without becoming bitter, depressed, rebellious or wallowing in self-pity?

Can we trust God enough to accept that whether He chooses to answer a prayer the way we want Him to answer it, or not, He who knows the future and knows everything, will cause everything to work out for my good?

He is my Father and He knows best, and He sometimes says "No!"

CHAPTER 16

HOPE

Never lose hope!

> "Faith is the substance of things hoped for, the evidence of things not seen." Hebrews 11:1

It struck me today as I was reading this verse that faith springs from HOPE. Putting the above verse a bit differently, the basis of our faith is hope, and if we have no hope, our faith has no substance! The building blocks of faith consist of HOPE. Faith is thus literally hope that has come alive; hope that has been transformed into active energy.

Without hope, we cannot believe, because hope is the kindling of faith, much as tiny twigs and thicker logs provide the kindling for a fire. It is hope that motivates us to keep on believing, often against the odds.

The day we lose hope, we lose the ability to believe. We cannot exercise faith for something we have no hope for! That's why it is so critical to never lose hope.

The Bible teaches us that faith comes by hearing the Word. The Word of God strengthens our faith and bolsters our confidence and conviction. Hope though is like the beacon of light that beckons you to come and draws your heart to the prospective joy of the outcome, the reward of your faith.

To have hope is to have a joyful anticipation of something good. If we lose that anticipation, that childlike expectation, our faith slips and loses its grip on that which we want to take hold of in the spiritual realm.

Never lose hope! Cling to it and keep it alive in your heart!

"But those who hope in the Lord will renew their strength. They will soar on wings like eagles; they will run and not grow weary, they will walk and not be faint." Isaiah 40:31

Chapter 17

The Dream

Don't ever lose hope! Cling to it even if there is nothing more to cling to.

- Hope is stronger than fear.
- It is stronger than failure;
- it is stronger than your inadequacy or ignorance;
- it is more powerful than any of your mistakes or wrong decisions!

In the fierce grip of hope, dreams are born. Dreams of spectacular things you've never even thought of. Dreams floating on the wings of hope and undeterred by reality. Driven by a fire in the furnace of faith in a God Who has no limitations and Who makes the impossible become possible.

In the wonder-world of dreams, vision is birthed.

Once the seed of a vision falls in soil ripened, prepared and fertilized by hope and dreams, there is no stopping the germination of passion and zeal in your soul. The young seedlings will sprout in your spirit and become giant trees.

Spurred on by passion, actions will follow and slowly the dream will find substance and become your reality. And, one day you wake up, and find yourself living the dream you refused to kill or let go or forget!

The dream, birthed in hope, flying on the wings of faith, has come to life!

CHAPTER 18

VICTORY IN THE WILDERNESS

Sometimes God allows us to go through trials and hardship. He allows us to enter seasons of barrenness, unfruitfulness; times where we feel we are travelling endless journeys through the wilderness. We go through seasons where we feel the heat of the sun scorching us every day and the cold stinging us every night; seasons where we feel that there is just no fruit. We don't hear the voice of God and it seems as though He has hidden His face from us; our prayers seem to drift unanswered through the heavens.

It is critical for our growth to maturity and our discovery of the depths of God that we don't give up in these times.

It is vital for our survival that we come to a place of victory there in the desert where we find ourselves. In such times we have to dig deeper and deeper within ourselves to find the Fountain of Life deep in our inner man; it is there in the wilderness, where there is nothing to be happy about, that we have to let our roots go deeper until we find the River of Joy that flows within us. Here in the wilderness of unfruitfulness, lack, loneliness, failure etc., we have to come to a place where we can say: "My soul WILL bless Thee oh Lord! My spirit WILL rejoice in You! I WILL magnify Your Name!"

Let praise come from your lips and exalt the Lord in the times when it is the most difficult to do so. Keep on praising and thanking Him until you find victory in the desert. Until there is only praise and gratitude in your heart and it doesn't matter anymore that you are barren; it doesn't matter that you have no water or food or success; it doesn't matter that things didn't work out.

All that matters is that He loves you; He wanted you; He chose you. You are His and He is yours!

Then you will rise up like an eagle and soar high above the hardship and difficulties! Then your breakthrough will come as the breaking of a new dawn as the Lord of Hosts fights your battles for you!

> "... for we live by faith, not by sight [living our lives in a manner consistent with our confident belief in God's promises] ... 2 Corinthians 5:7

$$-\cdot-$$

INTERLUDE

My poor health took a tremendous toll on our marriage. My husband, a very strong type A personality, could not deal with my illness at all. For a man who is used to fixing every problem and having answers for every challenge, it was impossibly difficult to deal with a problem he was unable to fix. He withdrew more and more and devoted all his time to the writing of books and recording of teachings and so forth.

I was alone in my room for the biggest part of every day. I felt myself spiralling deeper and deeper into a darkness that I had never known before. A darkness so dense it was almost a tangible, solid matter. At times I felt as if even God had deserted me and I was totally alone in this pitch-black hole of depression and pain. In desperation, I cried out to God for His intervention and He answered me. Though, not in the way, I had hoped He would answer me ...

One night, I had a particularly bad night with indescribable pain and slept fitfully and very little. I woke up very early in the morning and when I opened my eyes, I looked smack into the face of Jesus Christ...

The Encounter

I had made a cosy reading nook in the one corner of my bedroom with two lovely leather chairs and a beautiful lamp on a coffee table.

When I opened my eyes, He was sitting in one of those leather chairs. He had pulled the chair right up to my bed and sat watching me, with His chin resting on His hands. He looked at me like someone who had been patiently waiting for me to wake up.

What struck me the most about Him, was His eyes. There was a twinkle in His eyes that truly looked like stars! Love simply poured from His eyes! I have never experienced anything like that before. It was like being consumed with love. I melted in the presence of a Love so strong, so all-encompassing, so pure, so forgiving, so eternal.

All I could do was weep; completely undone by His presence ....

When I was able to look up again, I saw His mouth. He was grinning!! (Every time after this day when I saw Him, He seemed to be wearing this perpetual grin, like He was smiling all the time!) Through my tears I smiled at Him, unable to say a word or make a sound.

Eventually, I managed a word: "Lord..."

In that one word was encapsulated everything I wanted to say, everything I wanted to ask, every plea, every prayer. It seemed that words were not really necessary to communicate – He knew everything I wanted to say without me saying it.

Then He started talking. About all kinds of things – except my illness. (As I'm writing this, I am reminded of Job who also enquired from the Lord about his desperately painful situation, and after Job's friends gave up talking to him, he finally heard the voice of the Lord. God started speaking to Him about His creation and His omniscience; about the stars, the seas, the earth. He spoke to him about rain and thunderbolts and signs of the zodiac. He spoke to him about the clouds, lions, ravens and wild goats.

Everything except what he wanted to hear. (Job 38 to 41))

He taught me so many things. Sometimes I would ask a question and He would answer me and understanding and revelation just flooded my soul.

He visited me daily over the next few days. We spoke about so many things. Sometimes I asked Him to speak to me about a certain topic which I did not understand, and He would sit and teach me.

To be in His presence was indescribable. I do not have the vocabulary to describe the completeness, the utter satisfaction, the fullness of joy that one experiences in His presence. Truly the Psalm writer says in Psalm 16:11, "in His presence is fullness of joy!" There is no lack of anything. You do not want or need anything else. He is the total fulfilment of every desire and every need. Everything you could ever want is found in Christ!

I fell in love with Him utterly and completely. I became addicted to His presence. I started seeking Him in every moment; in every situation, even in the most mundane things. I wanted to never leave His presence. When I had to decide what to cook, I would ask Him – and He would answer me! When I woke up exhausted and couldn't think because my mind was so clouded with brain fog, I would ask Him, "Lord, what should I wear today?" And He would tell me what to wear!

I deliberately sought to be conscious of His presence every moment. I started conversing with Him about everything that was going on in my life. Literally, everything. My ears became attuned to His voice and I would often feel Him standing beside me and become aware of the Holy Spirit always being wherever He was. I learned to hear His voice when I was shopping for groceries, having coffee in a mall, driving past a homeless person.

Beloved, do you know that the God of the universe is interested in every single thing in your life? He is interested in whether you like a specific dress or not; He is interested in whether you desperately need to do a business deal to pay your mortgage! He is interested in what you're having for lunch and the appointment you have with a client. God wants to be a part of your life! He wants to be a part of your decision-making, your plans, your agendas. In Psalm 37:23 David writes, "He busies Himself with your every step!" Imagine that!

He loves talking to you and He loves that you talk to Him! This is what it means to have a relationship with God! Dear brother and sister, we don't have a religion – we have a relationship! In a relationship there is talking, sharing, listening, loving, crying, sometimes just sitting contentedly in one another's presence, joy, intimacy, etc. Everything you experience in a close relationship with someone, you can and should experience with God, just to a much greater degree.

I found myself at a place where I could hardly take a breath without Him on my mind. I was completely smitten with the beautiful Son of God! Like a user who tries crack cocaine for the first time and immediately becomes addicted, it took just one encounter with the Christ and I was 'hooked' forever.

After serving the Lord for more than 30 years, I now experienced Him on a total new level. My daily walk with Him entered a new dimension, and I began to understand a small measure of what it means when the Word of God speaks about Enoch who walked "in habitual fellowship with God," arm in arm; or what the scripture means when it says in Exodus 33:11, "And the Lord spoke to Moses face to face, as a man speaks to His friend."

CHAPTER 19

FACE TO FACE

Face to Face
with unveiled face I stand
drawn into the inner sanctum
by grace undeserved
division torn asunder
oneness becomes real
purchased by blood
so perfect and pure!
free to behold,
to look upon and gaze

Face to face...
unafraid in Your presence
understanding is opened.
the language of the heart
is spoken without words
knowledge becomes superfluous
the need to know redundant

Drowning in glory
words fall away
content in Your presence
my soul is at peace

in moments of oneness
the curtain is drawn
in awe, I behold as mysteries unfold
wondrous revelation
of stories untold.

No longer a riddle
the mirror obsolete
face to face
my love is complete

Years of desire
my soul yearning for Yours
consummated in love
inside the inner chamber
naked I stand
as layers fall away
all is revealed
all is known,
I am loved and accepted
by the Lover of my soul!

So the Lord spoke to Moses face to face, as a man speaks
to his friend." Exodus 33:11

CHAPTER 20

BONE OF MY BONE

From the depths of my soul
a love song arises
a passion to praise
a desire to sing

Deep calls unto deep
a longing to be one...
bone of my bone
and flesh of my flesh
my heart cries out
to be united with You!

The *Foretaste of things to come
a *Down payment so sweet!
ignites my heart and spurs me on
to seek You more
to want You more
my eyes are opened to behold
Your wondrous glory
lost in wonder at the depths of love reflected in Your eyes
enraptured in unspeakable delight
at Your smile and contagious laughter –
Jesus, Man of Joy!

I desire to be home –
where the temporal
is clothed by the eterna
where faith has finally been confirmed by sight
death is swallowed up in life
and darkness has disappeared in glory!

My heart cries out to be with You –
the One Whom I believe in ...
yet, have never seen!

*The Holy Spirit – the Promise of God. (Romans 8)

Chapter 21 The Dwelling Place of God

CHAPTER 21

THE DWELLING PLACE OF GOD

Psalm 22:3 says "He inhabits the praises of His people."

The word 'inhabit' means "to "dwell"; "to make His abode"; "make His camp"; "pitch His tent"; to "linger." There is a difference between "God living inside of us" and God actually "coming upon us" and "lingering" upon us. To linger means to "hang around"; to "stay awhile".

How amazing when God decides to linger a while!

In the Old Testament when the Israelites journeyed through the wilderness, the difference between His "presence with them" and His "glory upon them" was very clear. God was always "with" His people; the cloud travelled with them by day and the pillar of fire by night.

However, there were times when the presence of God would come down and totally envelop the tent of Moses. Other times Moses would walk up the mountain and the "glory" of the Lord would come down and Moses would literally be swallowed up in the glory of God. The Shekinah of God would fill the Tent of Meeting so that Moses could not enter.

When the Tabernacle of Solomon was completed, the Shekinah glory of God descended and filled the temple so that the priests could not stand because of the "weight" of His presence. That weighty presence of God is His "lingering" ... His glory, the kabod of God.

In the New Testament, we are the Temple; we are the tabernacle! The glory wants to "move in!" Not only does He desire to be with us, but He desires for His weighty presence, the kabod to make its abode within us.

He lives within us, yet we draw nearer to Him in praise.

We carry His Spirit in us, yet we enter deeper into Him and He into us when we worship Him.

It is in the moments of deep intimacy with Him that His weighty presence descends upon us and enfolds us like a blanket. It is for this that we were made. To live in His glory; to carry His glory, to wear the glory of God like a cloak.

Build a seat for Him through a life of praise. Let your worship rise to the heavens like incense until the kabod of God falls on you, lingers upon you, stays with you and transforms you effortlessly into His image.

Let your life become a habitation, a dwelling place for the living God.

Chapter 22

The Preciousness Laid Up for You

There is a preciousness in God that is not found in the letters and pages of the Bible.

It is found in the coolness of His touch as you sit in a breeze and watch the sunset. It is found in the sweetness of a smile that plays on your lips when, in an unexpected moment, He invades your thoughts; it is found in the choking back of tears when He shows you His goodness; the surprise of His presence when you open your eyes long before dawn … the sweetness of His kiss that lingers on your lips when you close your eyes in the midst of a chaotic day…

It is in the stirring of your emotions when you remember to focus on Him; the acceleration of your heartbeat when you look into His face … the wide-eyed wonder when you realize the God of the universe has just spoken to you …

These are the things that are not found in the letter of the Book, but these are the things that give life to the Word. This is the life-blood of the child of God. Without it, the Word remains simply words. Knowledge. Information.

This is the preciousness that is laid up for those whose heart is stayed on Him; the inheritance of him whose heart is wholly centred on God and whose eyes continually seek His face.

CHAPTER 23

LOOK INTO HIS FACE

How often in your day do you stop doing whatever it is that you're doing and just look up ... into the face of Jesus?

2 Corinthians 3:18 says: "... and we all with unveiled face, beholding as in a mirror, the glory of the Lord, are being transformed into the same image, from glory to glory just as from the Lord, the Spirit." (NKJV)

It is not in contending that we are changed; not in works or striving or discipline. Not in rigid observation of the law or mindless obedience. But it is there, in those moments where I simply look into His face. There, where I gaze upon His beauty and drink in His loveliness.

This scripture says we have to behold Him with "unveiled face." Not a face veiled with scepticism, prejudice, pride or fear, but unveiled. Brutally honest ... with a heart stripped of all pretence or performance or desire to impress.

It is there, in those moments, that we are transformed; changed into His very own image. There where His glory overshadows me, His presence overwhelms me. It is here that the layers that separate us are peeled away one after the other and He becomes part of me – Him in me, and me in Him.

Take a few moments in your day to meet with Him and just look into His face. If you're having a problem, cannot work something out, feel like you're 'losing it', just step into the secret place. Sit in His presence for a while and drink in His loveliness.

He's waiting there...

CHAPTER 24

MORE ON YIELDEDNESS

A heart that is completely yielded to God is focused on seeking God's will in every circumstance and determined to seek His heart in every situation. The reason for its very existence is solely to please the One to Whom he has surrendered his life.

So filled with this all-consuming desire to hear and obey the Master's voice is this heart, that there is simply no place for anything that does not befit the character of godliness.

This heart breaks at the slightest evidence of the fleshly sinful nature that still rears its head at times. The Spirit of God has free reign in his heart and is submissively allowed to test every motive, every meaning, every purpose and every attitude.

The heart that is so yielded and surrendered to God truly has eyes to see and recognize its weaknesses and hidden deceit as it mirrors itself in the Word; it has ears to hear the conviction of his Lord and great grace to crucify the flesh daily and live in the power of the resurrected Christ!

CHAPTER 25

REMAIN IN HIM

I was totally captivated by the glorious day; lost in childlike wonder at the splendour of His creation; marvelling at His goodness... and started my day enraptured by the indescribable beauty of my Lord... my Love...

Then it happened. I was plucked from His presence by an undeserved attack from my husband! I had the opportunity to be extremely angry and very upset and felt I had good reason to be.

My heart was broken. One moment I was there in His glory, overtaken by His presence, undone by His love, and the next moment I felt myself yielding to fierce anger and frustration.

Desperate for His presence, crying with disappointment, I started speaking to God: "Lord ..."

In a clear voice, He interrupted me: "Remain in Me ..." I started talking again, "But Lord ..." Once again, He interrupted me: "Lois, remain in Me ..."

Closing my eyes, I tried to shift my focus to find Him ... to find His presence again. And immediately I was there! His presence washed over me! His peace flooded my heart and drove out all anger and frustration from my mind. I was overwhelmingly aware of His presence again! What a precious lesson that was for me – His presence never leaves us! It is us, who step out of His presence! How reassuring then to know, that if you stepped out of or away from His presence, it takes just a moment, to step back into it.

Remain in Him and He will remain in you. Beloved, we have to practice remaining in His presence; we have to cultivate an awareness of the presence of Christ. Practising involves 'training'; doing something over and over until you can do it without any mistake.

And in the case of practising the awareness of Christ, it is simply a matter of directing your thoughts and your focus on Him.

Philippians 4:8-9 reads, "Finally brothers and sisters, whatever is true, whatever is noble, whatever is right, whatever is pure, whatever is lovely, whatever is admirable – if anything is excellent or praiseworthy – think about such things."

From this scripture, it is clear that one can (and should), decide or choose what you are going to think upon! And Paul helps us even further by telling us what to think upon.

Cultivate an awareness of His presence, and He will dwell and remain in you and upon you always

CHAPTER 26

LOVE IS THE GAME-CHANGER!

Your life will never change by setting goals for yourself that meet God's standard. We are unable to reach that standard in our own strength and with our own efforts. It is unattainable for us.

Remember every year's New Year's resolution?? We're not even able to do something like stop smoking or reading the Bible more in our own strength!

Our lives are changed when we discover what God has done for us. It is changed when we experience how much He loves us. We don't experience it when we manage to tick all the boxes of the law and manage to live a 'good life,' i.e. we go to church regularly, we tithe, we give to the poor and work at the soup kitchen, we get up at 06:00 every morning to read the Bible. No! No! No!!

We experience the love of God in the moments of our greatest weakness. In the shame and brokenness of having sinned. His love and forgiveness pour over us when we have fallen … again.

Judgement has never led anyone to victory. But love … now that is another story. Love that sees you at your worst moment and still feels nothing but love; a love that knows everything you have done, every secret thought and desire and still only loves...

That is what changes a life! An encounter with the mercy and grace of God. He draws us with His kindness and blows us away with His undeserved goodness and forgiveness; He woos us with His unfailing love until the day we step into His eternal Kingdom!

As we desire to change things in our own lives and as we introduce others to Jesus Christ, remember that we introduce them to Love. The One Who's love will never fail them; the One Who will never reject them;

Who will love them despite anything they might have done. The One Who's mercy is greater than any sin and Who's love will be the greatest motivator of all and the greatest enabler of all to be more like Him!

Mercy triumphs over judgement! Love is the game-changer; the Life-changer!

> "Or do you show contempt for the riches of His kindness, forbearance and patience, not realizing that God's kindness is intended to lead you to repentance?" Romans 2:4 NIV

CHAPTER 27

LET ME COUNT THE WAYS

I love how God loves us!

I love that He loves without prejudice; without any condition for His love.

I love how He loves without measure; without holding anything back, unreservedly.

I love how He loves so generously, superfluously, abundantly,

in shower upon shower of mercy, grace and kindness.

How great is your goodness that you have laid up for those who love You! How bountiful is Your mercy! How great is Your kindness! How immeasurable is Your grace! Eternal is Your love!

I love how He loves the unlovable.

I love how He chooses the outcasts of society and makes them belong.

I love how He takes sides with the underdog!

I love how He picks the rejected, the despised, the scorned and adopts them as His own.

I love how His heart beats for orphans and widows.

I love how He takes the lonely and becomes their greatest Companion.

I love how He sees the homeless and makes Himself their home ... their shelter ...

their hiding place ...

I love how He takes the one who doesn't belong and makes him part of a family.

I love how He takes him who was a nobody and makes him a somebody!

I love how He takes the humble and the lowly and raises them up to be counsellors to kings and rulers!

I love how He uses the foolishness of the world to confound the wise.

I love that He speaks for those who cannot speak!

I love how He defends the cause of the defenceless.

I love how He rules with justice and righteousness.

I love that He judges fairly!

I love how He extends grace to those who deserve it the least.

I love how He gives a second chance, a third chance and a fourth chance.

I love how He forgives my sins and never even thinks about them again.

I love that when He looks at me it is without the remembrance of everything I did wrong yesterday and the day before!

I love how He fixes that which is broken and doesn't throw it away!

I love how He helps me when I have fallen and doesn't rub my nose in the dirt!

How I love that He doesn't keep a record of all my wrongs.

I love how He looks at me through the blood of His Son and sees me perfect and holy and without spot or wrinkle. How grateful I am that He has faith in me when I have none.

I love that His love for me never changes, regardless of what I do (or don't do.)

I love that His love and acceptance of me is not based on how I performed today, but on how His Son performed on my behalf 2000 years ago!!

> "Oh give thanks to the Lord, for He is good; for His mercy
> and loving-kindness endure forever. Oh give thanks to the

God of gods, for His mercy and loving-kindness endure forever." Psalm 136: 1 & 2

CHAPTER 28

TRUSTING IN HIS CHARACTER

In times of trial and tribulation, testing and suffering, the greatest aim of satan is to cast a shadow on God in your mind. He purposefully works at sowing doubt, unbelief and resentment in our hearts toward God by planting questions such as "where is God?" "Why doesn't He hear when I call?" "He doesn't answer my prayers" "He doesn't provide for us," etc.

Constantly satan tries to twist the character of God in our perception.

If satan succeeds in making you doubt the character of God, he has dealt a severe, often fatal, blow to the foundation of your faith, making it almost impossible for you to trust God fully ever again.

Always be aware of this and remain unwavering in your belief that He is a good God; He is a loving God who cares for us beyond our understanding – even if everything in your circumstances is shouting out the contrary!

CHAPTER 29

DIVINE EXCHANGE

Once again, I find myself there ... naked before my God.

Unable to deny my weakness. Confronted by my complete inability to be what He wants me to be and to do what He wants me to be. Drowning in hopeless despair.

Facing the reality of who I am without Him:

- Not able to love
- Not able to forgive
- Not able to forget
- Not patient, not kind, not joyful!

Brokenness so intense tears me up and breaks my heart.

"Lord I can't ... I'm not able to ... I don't have the ability ... Help me, Lord ..."

I am wretched, naked, ashamed, guilty ... but for You.

In Your great love, You reached down and touched me. You grabbed a hold of my life never to let me go. In a heavenly romance You wooed me and courted me and made me Your own. In a divine exchange, You gave me Your name. All that You are have become mine – Your beauty, Your glory, Your strength, Your victory, Your righteousness.

My wretchedness was swallowed up in Your glory;
my nakedness was covered by Your robe of righteousness;
my sin and weakness forever washed away by Your great love.

My Lord and God ... How can I not pour out my life to You as a fragrant offering that exalts Your Name!

"O unhappy and pitiable and wretched man that I am! Who will release me from [the shackles of] this body of death? O thank God! [He will!] through Jesus Christ ..." Romans 7:24

CHAPTER 30

THE POWER OF SURRENDER

The greatest strength you will ever need is the strength to surrender your will, your abilities, your gifts and talents, your calling, and your choices to God.

There is nothing more difficult than the laying down of a will; nothing harder than choosing not to pick up a weapon. A weapon, the use of which you have mastered and honed to perfection. The ability to destroy your opponent with superbly-chosen words can destroy an ego or sting with sarcasm and humiliation worse than a whip.

There is probably nothing harder than not to resist or struggle or fight back when God wants you to surrender. Particularly when you know you have the ability to stand up and make an irrefutable argument for yourself!

Laying down your strength and choosing to be weak, is in all likelihood the most difficult thing you will ever be required to do. Allowing yourself to be vulnerable.

The way to strength is through weakness and vulnerability. It is impossible to reach a point of unwavering, immovable inner strength before you have allowed yourself, or sometimes deliberately chosen, the point of utmost vulnerability.

How have we become so blinded that we confuse strength, domination, intimidation and manipulation as 'strength', when Jesus Christ, our King and the Model upon Whom we mould our lives, says "Come and learn from Me for I am humble and lowly of heart."

In the book of Corinthians, the apostle Paul wrote the well-known and often quoted words, "...when I am weak, I am strong..." What a strange paradox that He says His strength is perfected in weakness. Paul was a powerful orator, yet he says his strength was perfected in weakness, and not displayed in strength and power and charisma!

It is in your weakness that you discover His grace; grace that is more than enough. You don't find God's grace when you are strong. You have to come to a place of lowliness; a place of weakness and a place of vulnerability to experience His grace.

"God resists the proud, but gives grace to the humble." James 4: 6

CHAPTER 31

DYING SOME MORE…

The message remains the same.
Every day.
Sometimes from moment to moment.

Lay yourself down.
Empty yourself of yourself.
And then empty yourself even more so that He can fill you.

It seems that I am so far away from empty that I will never reach it. Every day there is something that rears its head which I must then be emptied of.

What a paradox the Bible seems to present sometimes:

- empty yourself so that I can fill you
- give and you will receive
- sow and then you will reap
- be weak then you will be strong
- surrender and you will be victorious
- die and you will live

It seems that my whole life has become a process of dying. Although every day presents opportunities for me to stay alive and stay strong.

Frustration and irritation when I struggle with things;
Anger and despondency when I am in pain;
impatience with ignorant and incompetent staff in shops;
angry outbursts at the many people on the road who don't know how to drive!

Every day is filled with opportunities to get annoyed and irritated, good reasons to be impatient, full of yourself and strong in your own strength.

Yet time after time the words resonate in my heart: "Lay yourself down. You need to become less so that I can become more."

Will I ever master the art of dying completely when there is so much of myself still alive and strong and not willing to die?

The words of Dietrich Bonhoeffer reverberate through my being as I'm (still) walking this road of brokenness...

"When Christ calls a man, He bids him, come and die."

C.S. Lewis confirms this notion with his words: "Christ says, 'Give Me all. I don't want so much of your money and so much of your work; I want you. I have not come to torment your natural self, but to kill it."

Chapter 32

The Cost of the Anointing (Part 1)

How do I get an anointing?

I'm sure many preachers and Christian leaders have pondered this question! Wouldn't it be easy if we could just go into a shop and ask for a double-anointing? Something like a double-thick milkshake or a triple cheeseburger!

Yet, for most of us, the anointing is out of reach. Not because God doesn't want us to have it or because it's only reserved for certain people, but simply because it's just too expensive. We're not willing to pay the price.

Anointing does not come cheap. It does not simply expect a reasonable amount of your time, one, or even two chambers of your heart, or a good portion of your soul. It's certainly not happy to be on your priority list or part of your to-do list – "find the anointing!"

No! It is much more costly than that! Anointing wants everything or nothing! Anointing requires all of you. Everything you've got.

Anointing is not the same as gifting. You may be able to flow effortlessly in your gifting of prophecy, teaching or miracles, yet, without an anointing! Many Christian leaders mistakenly assume that their relationship with God is still good, or that God is pleased with them, just because He uses them or because the gifts of the Holy Spirit flow through them. This is a great deception! (My friend, God can use a donkey if He so wishes!)

The gifts and the calling of God are irrevocable, and if God has called you, He will continue to use you, even if you have become lukewarm, are backslidden or just going through the motions.

Don't fool yourself beloved! The anointing of God comes at a price! A very dear price!

It comes at the price of complete surrender. Surrender your own will, your ambitions, your dreams, your rights, etc.

It comes at the price of embracing His will and His predestined plan for you – with all the pain, heartache, loss or suffering that might include.

It will require not kicking against the goads of His guidance; a laying down of your own will and ideas and following His – with joy and gratitude!

The anointing is not for those who do not want to spend time seeking Him. It is not for those who do not long to be in His presence or to see Him face to face. Those who do not wish to hear His voice and know His face are in no danger to be graced with His powerful anointing.

CHAPTER 33

THE COST OF THE ANOINTING (PART 2)

There is no quick and simple way to obtain an anointing. There is no shop where you can run into and quickly buy an anointing.

In a time where everyone is looking for three easy steps to follow or instant results, there are no instant ways to "get it."

Anointing is the natural outflow of a life completely surrendered to Christ. It is the fruit that appears, as if by itself, in a person whose heart is set wholly upon God. It is not a reward, it's not anything you deserve or can work for.

Anointing is the manifestation of the presence of the Christ within you.

The more you die daily to yourself, the more visible and tangible Christ becomes in and through you. Note that the anointing is not reserved for a perfect person without any flaws, weaknesses or mistakes. Indeed, some of those who carry the greatest anointing might just be the ones who struggle the most to overcome their weaknesses and pitiful stumblings; one who clings to the mercy of his God.

Knowing the heart and character of his Father, he seeks Him until he finds Him, and clings to Him in desperate brokenness. His heart breaks over and over as he sits in the presence of His Lord where there is no condemnation, but instead, total love and complete acceptance. No (well-deserved) judgement, but rather encouragement and support.

The anointing requires brokenness; a pure and contrite spirit. A willingness to stand before your Maker, naked, and allow Him to search your heart, your mind, your soul, your thoughts, your motives, and not try to deny or hide or justify yourself. Just a bowing of your heart in sincere humbleness. Devoid of any self-righteous justification or arrogance. A heart that acknowledges its powerless efforts to overcome sin and a deep awareness of the price that was paid for that sin. Yet, at the same time, an unshakable faith that you have been forgiven, cleansed and forever accepted into the family of God.

Such a revelation leaves one speechless in wonder at His immeasurable kindness and grace; lost for words at a love so great. No words could ever express the overwhelming gratitude for such a great price paid on your behalf. In the presence of Love, there is a breaking of your spirit and a crushing of your heart that takes place. Not a breaking with the intent to destroy, but rather to awaken to the Christ-life. A breaking that opens your eyes to see and your mind to gain understanding.

Such an encounter with God leaves you changed forever. It births within you an insatiable hunger for God that drives you to seek Him more and more. There is a thirst within you and a need to be in God's presence constantly, and it cannot be quenched by attending meetings, conferences, church gatherings, etc. This need is for Him! They need to see His face, to look upon His beauty, to see His smile, to feel His presence and be soaked with His glory. When you rise from such an encounter with God you are filled with His presence; you carry His presence; His glory; His anointing.

The difference between anointing and charisma or knowledge of a subject, or good oratory skill is vast! While it could be interesting, informative and "nice to listen to", these contain no power to change a heart at all. Knowledge combined with charisma is a powerful tool that can draw the crowds and wow the masses – yet, it is only the Word of God that can transform a life. It is only an encounter with the living Christ in a person carrying His anointing, which can grab hold of those held captive in darkness and launch them into the Kingdom of light and glory!

> "When Thou didst say, seek My face, my heart said, "Thy face will I seek." Psalm 27:8

CHAPTER 34

— · —

THE COST OF THE ANOINTING (PART 3)

THE WONDER OF THE TRINITY

In the previous writing about the cost of the anointing, I stated the following: The anointing is the natural outflow of a life completely surrendered to Christ. It is the fruit that appears, as if by itself, in a person whose heart is set upon God, and follows hard after God. Anointing is the manifestation of the presence of the living Christ within you.

How precious is this truth in the light of scripture such as is found in Song of Solomon 1:3, where the bride calls out at the Groom, "Your Name is as ointment (perfume) poured forth."

In Psalm 107:20 David writes prophetically, "He sends forth His Word and heals them..." Jesus Christ as the Living Word is the embodiment of this prophetic word!

In Jeremiah 8:22, the writer asks: "Is there no balm in Gilead? Is there no physician there? Why then is not the health of the daughter of my people restored? [Because Zion no longer enjoyed the presence of the Great Physician!) One of the Names of God is Jehovah Rapha – The Lord your healer. Jesus is the Balm of Gilead, Who poured out His life as a sacrifice for mankind.

When one speaks about the anointing, however, one speaks about such a multi-faceted and multi-layered truth, which demands more in-depth exploration.

In Luke 4:16-21 we find the account in scripture where Jesus stood up in the temple to read. He opened the scroll to Isaiah 61:1-2, which reads: "The Spirit of the Lord is upon Me, because He has anointed Me to preach the good news to the poor; He has sent Me to announce release to the captives and recovery of sight to the blind, to send forth as delivered those who are oppressed; to proclaim the accepted and acceptable year of the Lord. V20 Then He rolled up the book and gave it back to the attendant and sat down; and the eyes of all in the synagogue were gazing attentively at Him. V21 And He began to speak to them: Today this scripture has been fulfilled while you are present and hearing."

Clearly, He was speaking about the Holy Spirit, and saying that He, the Christ, was anointed by the Holy Spirit of God. Obviously, Jesus could not anoint Himself, so He was anointed by the Holy Spirit.

Now, no longer are we saying that Christ within us is the anointing, but the Holy Spirit on us, in us and upon us is our anointing!

When we research the Hebrew meaning of the word 'anoint,' we find that it means, to smear or rub with oil, typically as part of a religious ceremony. Or, to ceremonially confer a divine or holy office upon (a priest, or monarch), by smearing or rubbing with oil.

Wikipedia offers the following definition: Anointing is the ritual act of pouring oil over a person's head or entire body. By extension the term is also applied to related acts of sprinkling, dousing or smearing a person or object with any perfumed oil, milk, butter, or other fat.

The example that comes to mind immediately, is of course King David who was anointed as king over Israel by the prophet Samuel. In 1 Samuel 16 the event is chronicled in Verses 12 and 13: "Then the Lord said, "Rise and anoint him; he is the one." So Samuel took the horn of oil and anointed him in the presence of his brothers, and from that day on the Spirit of the Lord came upon David in power..."

Further research of the word 'anoint,' leads us to the Hebrew, Yeshua Hamashiach, which of course means, 'The Anointed One' or Messiah in Greek.

In our scripture in Luke 4:16-21, Jesus Himself declares that He has been anointed by God, to fulfil His mission. (This was of course the fulfilment of the prophecy by the prophet Isaiah.) In this context, we have to remember, that Jesus did all His miracles, every wonder, as a man, filled and baptised by the Holy Spirit, and not as God the Son. All His works were done as an ordinary man, under the anointing of the Holy Spirit and by faith in His Father Who sent Him.

Thus, we can say, that the anointing is God's enablement for us to fulfil our calling and execute our mission. Without the anointing, we will not be able to accomplish any of the things God requires us to do. Indeed, Isaiah 10:27, states, "....The yoke shall be destroyed because of fatness which prevents it from going around your neck."

In the scripture above, the word 'fatness' refers to oil, (as being anointing oil.) The relation between 'fatness' and 'oil' is an obvious one. Oil is often used in scripture in context with the Holy Spirit, and we can assuredly say that the anointing is the anointing of and by the Holy Spirit. According to this scripture, we need the anointing to break yokes. No yoke of sickness can be broken without the anointing; no yoke of slavery, poverty or captivity. We desperately need the anointing!

So, is the anointing then of the Holy Spirit, or is it the manifestation of Christ within us? Are these in conflict with one another? Most certainly not!

Brothers and sisters, here is where the wonder and mystery of the Trinity enter the equation! In John 17:21, Jesus prays to the Father and says, "Father I pray that they all may be one, as You, Father, are in Me, and I in You; that they also may be in Us, so that the world may believe that You sent Me."

Whilst it is true, that the Trinity are three different Persons and have different functions, They can never be separated from One another. They never work independently from One another! Where the Father is, there is the Son, there is the Spirit! They are all One in One another. A beautiful example of this can be seen in Genesis in the story of creation. In Chapter 1:2 we read, "The earth was without form and an empty waste, and darkness was upon the face of the very great deep. The Spirit of God was moving (hovering, brooding) over the face of the waters. And God (the Father) said, (the Word!) Let there be light; and there was light." The Holy Spirit hovered over the waters, fertilizing and incubating the deep, the Father commissioned, the Son, (the Word), executed the command! All three Persons were actively involved in the same mission!

A vivid account of Jesus' involvement in Creation is also found in Proverbs 8:27-31. Jesus, Who is the Wisdom of God, is speaking of Himself in this account, as 'Wisdom.'

> "When He prepared the heavens, I [Wisdom], was there; when He drew a circle upon the face of the deep and stretched out the firmament over it. V28 When He made firm the skies above, when He established the fountains of the deep, v29 when He gave to the sea its limit and His decree that the waters should not transgress [across the boundaries set by] His command, when He appointed the foundations of the earth v30 Then I [Wisdom], was beside Him as a master and director of the work; and I was daily

> His delight, rejoicing before Him always. V31 Rejoicing in His inhabited earth and delighting in the sons of men."

Another beautiful example is found in the New Testament where Jesus is baptized by John the Baptist. In Matthew 3 we see the Son of God walking into the Jordan River to be baptized; we hear the Father declaring from heaven, "This is My Son in Whom I am well pleased," and we see the Holy Spirit ascending upon Jesus in the form of a dove. How beautiful and marvellous is our God! The Trinity of God, unique in Person and function, yet completely One.

Therefore, when one speaks of the Holy Spirit, the spirit of Christ, Who proceeded from the Father, is inseparably included in that reference, and it is in no way contradictory to one another.

After Jesus was baptized, the Holy Spirit led Him into the desert where He was tempted and tested for 40 days and 40 nights. After He overcame, He went back to Galilee and settled in Capernaum, and commenced His mission.

Chapter 35

The Cost of the Anointing Part 4)

For a better understanding of the cost of the anointing, we need to understand what the anointing is, and what exactly it will mean for us personally if we want a greater anointing. Yes, there is a cost to the anointing. Yes, there is a price to pay to obtain the anointing. Sure, the gospel is free and the salvation of God in Jesus Christ is a free gift of God to mankind. Rightly the scripture says in Matthew 10:8 "...freely you have received, freely give."

However, there are levels of service to God, after salvation, which are only obtained by sacrifice and consecration. There are still 'prices' of consecration to be paid by every believer.[1] (This is NOT to be understood as works that need to be performed by believers in order to be given the anointing as a reward. As Christians, we do not have a works-based religion, but a love (and grace) filled relationship.)

Nevertheless, take a look at what Jesus Himself said in Matthew 16:24: "Then Jesus said to His disciples, if anyone desires to be My disciple, let him deny himself, and take up his cross and follow Me."

In the days of Jesus, if you saw someone carrying a cross, you knew he was a 'dead man walking.' Within a matter of minutes or hours, this person would be nailed to a cross and die. For us, to take up our cross means the same thing. We are to be 'a dead man walking.' We are to live a life where we continuously deny ourselves; deny our rights; lay down our position, our title, our expectations, our right to be right, etc., etc. The list is endless. I would say that that is quite a steep price to pay!

To become a child of God is free and easy; to become a follower or a disciple of Jesus Christ, is costly!

This is confirmed in Luke 9:62, where again we find Jesus speaking about the cost of following Him: "And Jesus said to him, "No one, having put his hand to the plough and looking back, is fit to be called my disciple."

In the Bible, Kings, Prophets and Priests were anointed by a specific anointing oil, so as to consecrate them for their specific office. Taking a look at Exodus 30:22-25, we will see what the anointing oil was made of in the Old Testament. We gain much understanding when we study this, and see what each one of these ingredients means regarding the cost to be anointed.

> "Moreover, the Lord said to Moses, take the best spices: of liquid myrrh 500 shekels, of sweet-scented cinnamon half as much, 250 shekels, of fragrant calamus, 250 shekels, and of cassia 500 shekels and of olive oil a hin. And you shall make of these a holy anointing oil, a perfume compounded after the art of the perfumer; it shall be a sacred anointing oil."

Each one of these ingredients was very valuable, rare and costly. Note that the Lord told Moses to use the best spices – not spices of inferior quality nor spices that were commonly found! In verse 32 we read, "It shall not be poured upon a layman's body, nor shall you make any other like it in composition; it is holy, and you shall hold it sacred." Wow! So, this oil was not to be used for just anybody but only for those consecrated to God, and it could not be duplicated or faked by anything similar in composition! How easily the masses are fooled today by a "fake anointing!" How often charisma, hype and good entertainment are used as a substitute for the anointing of God!

> Brokenness and sorrow are portals that give you access to dimensions in God that you would never otherwise be able to enter into. Lois van Heerden

[1] Credit to Christine Darg from whom I have borrowed some and adapted others.

CHAPTER 36

—·—

THE ANOINTING OIL

Let's look again at the scripture in Exodus which describes the anointing oil:

> "Moreover, the Lord said to Moses, v23 Take the best spices: of liquid myrrh 500 shekels, of sweet-scented cinnamon half as much, 250 shekels, of fragrant calamus 250 shekels, v24 and of cassia 500 shekels, in terms of the sanctuary shekel and of olive oil a hin. v25 and you shall make of these a holy anointing oil, a perfume compounded after the art of the perfumer; it shall be a sacred anointing oil."

The holy anointing oil described in Exodus 30:22–25 was created from:

- Pure myrrh (מר דרור mar deror) 500 shekels (about 6 kg)
- Sweet cinnamon (קינמון בשם kinnemon besem) 250 shekels (about 3 kg)
- "fragrant cane" (קְנֵה-בֹשֶׂם qaneh-bosem, sometimes translated as calamus) 250 shekels (about 3 kg)
- Cassia (קדה kiddah) 500 shekels (about 6 kg)
- Olive oil (שמן זית shemen zayit) one hin (about 6 litres, or 5.35 kg)

The first ingredient of the anointing oil was myrrh. Myrrh is a fragrance that comes from the trunk of the Commiphora tree found in Arabia, and it is produced in the form of tears from the trees. Alcohol is added to remove any impurities, and then it is steamed. As the steam passes through the gum, it's melted into oil, and that oil becomes a perfume.

Myrrh can be seen as a symbol of meekness formed through difficulties, hardship and trials as can be seen in the tears of the Commiphora tree.

The second ingredient of the anointing oil was cinnamon. Cinnamon comes from a tree that grows 30 to 40 feet, and it grows remarkably straight.

The description of cinnamon in the Hebrew language means "sweet." The fruit and the leaves of the tree were squeezed and bruised until the spicy, sweet oil dripped from the paste. The most pungent of the spice, however, was obtained from the bark of the tree.

The finest grade of cinnamon comes from the inner bark of the tree, which is obtained from the tree by making incisions with a sharp knife, on both sides of the branch. The fruit and the coarse pieces of bark are then boiled and yields a fragrant, sweet oil.

The third ingredient of the holy, anointing oil, was calamus, a reed that grows in swamps. The head of the reed is filled with oil, and you knew it was ready for the picking when the head of the reed was bent over almost in half, with the weight of the oil. When the wind blew over the calamus, a sweet fragrance was released and carried on the breeze. When it is dried and pulverized, the Calamus yields a very fine, aromatic smell, and when reduced to powder it forms an ingredient in the most precious perfumes.

Growing in such lowly surroundings as a muddy swamp, Calamus teaches us about humility, in the same way, that Jesus Christ voluntarily left His heavenly abode and chose to make His home among the children of men – releasing His sweet perfume among mankind when He was battered, bruised and pulverized to such an extent that He wasn't even recognizable as a man. (Isaiah 53)

The fourth ingredient in the anointing oil was called cassia. Cassia produces a leaf called senna. Cassia is an aromatic bark, similar to cinnamon, but differing in strength and quality. Cassia bark is darker, thicker and coarser, and the corky outer bark is often left on. The outer surface is rough and greyish-brown, the inside bark is smoother and reddish-brown. Cassia is less costly than cinnamon and is often ground as cinnamon. When bought as sticks, cinnamon rolls into a single quill while cassia is rolled from both sides toward the centre so that they end up resembling scrolls.

The ingredient of cassia reminds us of the suffering Servant Who was the sacrifice for the sins of the world.

The brokenness of His body was the sweet fragrance to the Father that He had won the human race back to Himself (Ephesians 4:8).

The likeness and similarities between the anointing oil and Jesus Christ Himself are none less than remarkable. He is found in every ingredient in the Holy oil.

In the myrrh, He is found as the personification of meekness. In His own words in Matthew 11:29 Jesus said: "Take My yoke upon you and learn of Me, for I am gentle (MEEK) and HUMBLE (lowly) in heart and you will find rest..."

In the cinnamon, He is found as the sweet rose of Sharon and the perfume poured out in His Name in the Song of Solomon. "[And she continues] The odour of your ointment is fragrant; your name is like perfume/ointment poured out ..." Song of Solomon 1:3.

In the Calamus, He is found as the rod (reed) of Jesse Who is bruised and beaten to an unrecognizable pulp. "There shall come forth a Rod from the stem of Jesse, and a Branch out of his roots shall bear fruit." Isaiah 11:1.

> "... He has no form or comeliness (royal, kingly pomp) that we should look at Him, and no beauty that we should desire Him." Isaiah 53: 2b

In the fourth ingredient, Cassia, He is portrayed as the humble servant of God. Jesus' entire life and ministry were characterized by humility and servanthood. Many examples of this can be found in the scripture but probably none more powerful than in John 13, 14 and 15. Christ the Servant Leader.

Read on to find out the profound symbolic meaning of the olive oil .... the fifth ingredient ...

> Submission and meekness is the wild, untamed, powerful stallion, submitting to the bit, the bridal, the saddle, and the tug of the reins. Jentezen Franklin

CHAPTER 37

THE OLIVE PRESS

The fifth and last ingredient of the anointing oil was a hin of olive oil (about 5 ½ - 6 litres).

While the other four ingredients added spice, sweetness and fragrance, the olive oil was the "carrier oil." The substance that "carried" all of the above. The myrrh, the cinnamon, the calamus, the cassia were all mixed into the carrier oil. The olive oil thus carried the meekness, the sweetness, the fragrance, the humility. Not one of the ingredients in the anointing oil was obtained without extreme bruising, crushing, pounding, pulverizing pressure!

The name Gethsemane means The Olive Press. How apt a place for our Redeemer to spend His last agonizing hours where his sweat would turn to blood!

Gethsemane was a garden in which many olive trees were found. In order to harvest the precious oil from the olive fruit, the olive tree was fiercely shaken and beaten with poles to shake all the olives loose from the tree. The oil was then extracted with a mortar and pestle or grounded by a stone press made of solid rock. (Exodus 27:20; Deut: 33:24) After being pounded into a pulp it was subjected to even more pressing.

The beaten oil (Exodus 27:20; 29:40) was made by bruising in a mortar.

After being beaten, bruised, crushed, pounded into an unrecognizable mass, the pulp was then poured into wicker baskets, from which the finest, purest of the oil could easily run off. This oil was known as the beaten oil.

The remainder of the pulp was (and is) then used to make delicious, healthy olive pastes, pate's, tapenades etc., which is an expensive and sought-after delicacy all over the world.

Bearing the above in mind, let us now read the scripture in Isaiah 53 and 54 and notice the remarkable resemblance between the journey of the olive fruit and that of our Lord Jesus Christ. Can there be any doubt that Christ Himself was also the anointing oil used for the anointing of His servants; the healing oil sent to heal; the sweet fragrance that emanates from a child of God walking in oneness with Him; the humility that is the most outstanding character trait of a true servant of God?

[2]For He shall grow up before Him as a tender plant,
And as a root out of dry ground.
He has no form or comeliness;
And when we see Him,
There is no beauty that we should desire Him.
[3]He is despised and rejected by men,
A Man of sorrows and acquainted with grief.
And we hid, as it were, our faces from Him;
He was despised, and we did not esteem Him.
[4]Surely He has borne our griefs
And carried our sorrows;
Yet we esteemed Him stricken,
Smitten by God, and afflicted.
[5]But He was wounded for our transgressions,
He was bruised for our iniquities;
The chastisement for our peace was upon Him,
And by His stripes we are healed.
[6]All we like sheep have gone astray;
We have turned, every one, to his own way;
And the LORD has laid on Him the iniquity of us all.
[7]He was oppressed and He was afflicted,
Yet He opened not His mouth;
He was led as a lamb to the slaughter,
And as a sheep before its shearers is silent,
So He opened not His mouth.
[8]He was taken from prison and from judgment,
And who will declare His generation?
For He was cut off from the land of the living;
For the transgressions of My people He was stricken.
[9]And they made His grave with the wicked—
But with the rich at His death,
Because He had done no violence,
Nor was any deceit in His mouth.
[10]Yet it pleased the LORD to bruise Him;
He has put Him to grief.
When You make His soul an offering for sin,
He shall see His seed, He shall prolong His days,

And the pleasure of the LORD shall prosper in His hand.
[11]He shall see the labor of His soul, and be satisfied.

Isaiah 53 NKJV

— · —

POSTLUDE

I wish I can say that I am healed today, but I can't.

For reasons that I don't know or understand, God has chosen not to heal me, and my health remains a daily struggle. Many well-known preachers with wonderful healing ministries have prayed for me, and almost without exception, I felt the presence of God come upon me and would return home exhilarated and full of faith, only to be disillusioned after a few days of "walking in faith," "accepting my healing in faith," when the pain would cripple me once again.

Why do some people get healed and others not?

The short answer is, I don't know. Over the years this question has been the topic of debate for many church leaders. Many 'explanations' are offered that sound right and reasonable and certainly are true in some cases, yet, we have to admit that there are those cases that we simply cannot explain or understand. The many cases where people truly trusted God and truly believed; where hundreds or sometimes thousands of prayers were offered up to beseech God for the life or health of a person, and still the person passed away or remained sick.

Does that change my belief that God is a God Who heals and restores and wants to make us whole? Absolutely not! The Word of God is very clear in Isaiah 53 that Jesus bought healing for us, where it says in verse 5, "But He was wounded for our transgressions, He was bruised for our guilt and iniquities;...and with the stripes that wounded Him we are healed and made whole." God desires for us to be healthy and prosperous. It is His desire that we are blessed and that it goes well with us. This is confirmed over and over in the scripture, both the Old and New Testaments.

In 3 John 2 the Apostle John writes, "Beloved, I pray that you may prosper in all things and be in health, just as your soul prospers."

> The entire life and ministry of Jesus Christ demonstrated God the Father's will for us, namely to be healed, to be set free, to be made whole, to be delivered. He came as God in the flesh to make the Father known to us, and He did so in such a way that we can have no doubt about God's will at all. Wherever He went He healed the sick, drove out demons, brought liberty to those held in captivity!

It is my humble opinion however, we can never 'overrule' or leave God's sovereignty out of the equation when discussing this topic. God is God and He can do whatever He wants. He is Lord and Creator of all and in His sovereignty, He can make decisions that we cannot necessarily understand or explain.

It needs to be said that no action (or lack of action) on God's part needs to be understood by us as His children.

Not once in the Bible does it say we have to understand God, yet, it says over and over we have to believe in Him and trust in Him.

We will never understand everything that has happened or why God did not intervene in some event as long as we are on earth, and we have to accept that. In 1 Corinthians 13:9, the scripture says that "... our knowledge is fragmentary (incomplete and imperfect) ....and again in verse 12, "For now we are looking in a mirror that gives only a dim (blurred) reflection [of reality as in a riddle or enigma], but then [when perfection comes] we shall see in reality and face to face! Now I know in part (imperfectly), but then I shall know and understand fully and clearly, even in the same manner as I have been fully and clearly known and understood [by God]."

If it was so that we could fully understand and explain the ways of God, He could not be God. If we were able to explain and clarify everything God does and does not do, we would be guilty of bringing God down to our own level of humanity and we simply cannot do that. In the relation of man to God, there has to be that element of mystery and inexplicability, otherwise man and God would be equal.

Romans 11 verses 33 and 34 sum it up well: "Oh, the depths of the riches and wisdom and knowledge of God! How unfathomable (inscrutable, unsearchable) are His judgements (His decisions)! And how untraceable (mysterious, undiscoverable) are His ways (His methods, His paths)! For who has known the mind of the Lord and who has understood His thoughts, or who has (ever) been His counselor?"

Somewhere in the middle of 2016, my medical aid agreed to pay for me for an evaluation for physical rehabilitation. Even though the report by the clinic reinforced the fact that I desperately needed rehabilitation to restore my mobility, range of motion etc., the medical aid refused to pay for the treatment and we simply did not have the finances. Our family in Christ made quick work of the cost and within a day or two, I received the full payment of the expenses and more.

The rehabilitation proved to be a life-saving intervention for me.

Because of the fact that I had become almost bedridden in 2015 and 2016, I had to undergo extensive therapy to restore my mobility. Most of my muscle tissue had simply disappeared over the last 18 months and the smallest movement had become difficult for me. The physiotherapists and bio-kineticists were absolutely amazing though, and slowly my body started to win back the motion and mobility I had lost – millimetre by small millimetre.

Like a small child, I had to learn to walk properly again, place my feet correctly, restore my balance, my posture, and most of all my confidence. In retrospect, I believe that I would have been bound to a wheelchair if I had not undergone that treatment at that critical time.

In January 2018 I finally underwent major back surgery, after I had changed to another medical aid.

Clinically the surgery was a success, although I still experienced nerve pain, but not to the same degree as before the surgery. In most cases, recovery after back surgery takes time, and in my case, it was no different.

Weeks of invaluable rehabilitation followed once again. Slowly my life returned to some form of normalcy again, and I was able to go out on my own, have coffee with a friend or attend a gathering of believers.

Around the beginning of 2019, the pain returned, sometimes as severe as it had been before my operation. Once again seeking answers I learned that my muscles went into spasms that were extremely painful. I was also given a back brace to wear, to support my spine.

Around the middle of 2019, I was diagnosed with rheumatoid arthritis, a debilitating auto-immune disease.

I was devastated.

Not only did I now have to fight degenerative osteoarthritis, but a possibly crippling disease for which, as yet, there is no cure.

Through my writings, it is clear that I believe that there is sometimes suffering that is allowed by God. Such suffering I believe has to be embraced and accepted and allowed to do the work in you that God wants to accomplish. In her precious book, Hinds feet on High Places, Hanna Hurnardt writes a compelling story about the purpose and the power of sorrow and suffering to change the child of God into His image daily. In the book of James 1: 2, 3 & 4, the Apostle James confirms the fact that trials, testing and tribulation are powerful tools in the hands of God to change us. Bear in mind that God's purpose with His children, more than anything else, is for us to conform to the image and character of Christ! As much as He loves to bless and to prosper His children, these things are always secondary to the purpose of moulding us into the image and glory of His Son!

Does this mean that I just accept willingly any attack of the enemy on my physical well-being, relationships, finances, etc? Absolutely not! No onslaught of the devil upon a child of God should ever be accepted or tolerated, but should be rebuked, resisted, and refused with all the authority we have in Jesus Christ! However, there has to be distinguished between an assault of the enemy, and a trial that is allowed by God which needs to be embraced.

Do I wish to be completely healed? Of course! Do I still trust God for my healing? For sure!

Over the course of the last few years, something has changed, however. The greatest thing I pursue is not my health and healing. Praying for healing is not the main topic of my prayers. My conversations with God do not solely revolve around being healthy.

The greatest quest in my life has become to know Him!

He is the Love of my life; the Lover of my soul! There is nothing I want more than to be with Him. When I am with Him, it seems like everything else pales in comparison to the absolute glory of His presence. To talk to Him about healing me when I sit with Him almost seems trivial sometimes. I have discovered the very Essence of Life;

- The Life-Giver Himself;
- The Joy-giver;
- The One in Whose presence is fullness of joy.
- The One Who makes my cup run over!

Everything I want and desire is in Him! When my mind is stayed on Him and my heart is focused on Him, I am truly not even aware of pain in my physical body – all my senses are filled with Him!

- My eyes behold His beauty;
- My ears hear His voice;
- I get drunk with His fragrance of roses, spikenard, myrrh and other indescribable fragrances;
- With my hands, I touch His face and caress Him like a woman who caresses the love of her youth. With my mouth I kiss Him and taste His sweetness.

I am completely fulfilled in Him and totally surrendered to His plan and will for my life. I trust Him implicitly and know that whatever He has destined for me will be good. I take great comfort from scriptures like Romans 8:28, "And we know [with great confidence] that God [who is deeply concerned about us] causes all things to work together [as a plan] for good for those who love God, to those who are called according to His plan and purpose."

Whilst I do not yet have answers and understanding for my circumstances, I derive immense hope and joy from the Word of God, as is written in Romans 8:38: "I am convinced that nothing can ever separate us from God's love. Neither death nor life, neither angels nor demons, neither our fears for today nor our worries about tomorrow – not even the powers of hell can separate us from God's love."

Chapter 38

Called To Be With Him

God desires intimacy with His sons and daughters. He desires friendship. He desires a relationship of love.

Oft times our relationship with God is reduced to merely praying for our needs or crying out for our crises. Sometimes all we do is ask; for provision; for protection; for breakthrough; for blessing.

Of course, there is nothing wrong with bringing our needs to God. In fact, He invites us to do so. But when our walk with God has been reduced to merely praying for our outcome, blessing on everything we do, provision etc., we are missing the most important and most glorious privilege of being a child of God, and that is to have close and intimate fellowship with our Creator.

We were made first and foremost, to be with Him. To talk to Him; to share our lives with Him; to listen to Him and let Him talk to us, teach us, guide us, laugh with us and dance with Him.

Mark 3:14: "He appointed the twelve, whom He named apostles. He wanted them to be continually at His side as His friends, and so that he could send them out to preach and have authority to heal the sick and cast out demons."

CHAPTER 39

WHO SHALL BE MY RESTING PLACE

I was so blessed by the scripture in Zacharia where we read where the Lord asks the question: "Who shall be My resting place?"

He doesn't ask, "Where shall be My resting place?" but 'who' shall be My resting place. God is seeking a resting place in you and me.

We all know that He lives within us and is always with us, but a resting place is something quite different. A resting place speaks of "making a permanent residence;" "It means to make a home;" "it means to dwell."

In the Old Testament, we see such good examples of God coming down in a cloud and coming to rest upon Moses' tent or enveloping Moses and Joshua in Himself.

The New Testament is a better covenant, in which we have the indwelling of the Holy Spirit within us all the time. We have become content with knowing that God lives on the inside of us, although most of the time we forget that the Creator is inside us!

What this scripture refers to is the "weighty presence of God;" the 'kabod' of God. Not only does He want to live inside of us, but He wants us to carry His weighty presence wherever we go! His kabod! His glory!

In the New Testament in the book of 1 Corinthians 6:9, the apostle Paul rightly asks the question: "What? know ye not that your body is the temple of the Holy Ghost which is in you, which ye have of God, and ye are not your own?" (I particularly like this translation in the King James Bible because I can just hear Paul's shocked surprise when he asks the question "What?" In my modern-day English I would probably write: "Whaaaat???? Don't you know that your body is the house of God and that He lives inside of you? What is wrong with you people? How can you sin with your body knowing that Jesus Christ lives inside you?"

I'm taking up the challenge anew this morning to become a resting place for God and become a carrier of His presence – what about you?

CHAPTER 40

RISKY LOVING

Truly loving someone asks you to reveal your most vulnerable self to that person.

Not holding anything back; not having any secrets; not trying to be someone you are not. Taking the risk that when that person really knows who you are, you will still be loved, still accepted, still celebrated.

Much courage is needed to be so completely vulnerable. Love is required that is greater than any fear of being hurt, rejected, weighed and found 'not good enough to love.'

Love is the greatest power in the world; the strongest force. True love is not scared of being hurt because love is so much stronger than hurt or pain. True love is able to love despite being rejected or hurt.

Can such a love actually be found?

The answer is a resounding yes! There is a true love that is being demonstrated for the last 2000 years. A love that was willing to leave a glorious kingdom behind and be willing to be born as a mortal man. To be raised in the home of a poor family and work with His hands to make a living.

So great and all-encompassing was this love that it was willing to be rejected, despised, cursed, spat upon, mocked and nailed to a wooden cross for the sake of the very people who killed Him. Such was the nature of this pure love that it was willing to take the ultimate risk and die for His beloved, without having any guarantee that ultimately, she will return His love. A love that was not only willing but desired to die for the one He loved.

A calculated risk one might say. But I would say, a risk that could not afford not to be taken.

Such is the nature of true love ... I love you even if you don't love me; I accept you – even if you hate me.

Truthfully, there is no risk in that, because I cannot help myself. Love covers all! Love covers a multitude of sins.

Love is greater than the greatest offence, and the joy I find in loving you, supercedes any sacrifice required on my part!

CHAPTER 41

IN THE PRESENCE OF MY ENEMIES

My heart and mind are filled with Psalm 23 this morning and specifically verse 5.

Take a look at verse 4, which says, "even though I walk through the valley of the shadow of death, I will fear no evil, for you are with me. Thy rod and thy staff they comfort me... v5 You prepare a table before me in the presence of my enemies..."

Note that He lays a table for you after you've come through the valley. You might be walking through a valley of great despair and what feels like total darkness ... but, there's a table waiting for you when you come through on the other side of the valley. This is a table of victory! A table laden with delicacies fit to celebrate!

"Preparing a table" means that great care is taken to set the table just right, that it is beautiful and inviting. It speaks of a meal that is waiting; nourishment; new strength, new energy. "Preparing" also indicates that care is taken with what food is prepared and how it is prepared, that it can be served at its most delicious and precisely the right time.

God chooses to lay a table before us, right after we've come through the valley. When we are weary of battle, tired, exhausted beyond words; when we don't have the strength to go on; and our enemies are mere onlookers and defeated spectators as we enjoy the feast He has prepared for us.

And He doesn't stop there! No! After we've been nourished with food from heaven, He anoints my head with oil. Oil in the Bible is almost always a reference to the Holy Spirit. Oil was used to anoint those chosen by the Lord for a specific function or office; it was used to cleanse and refresh; it was symbolical of a clothing in authority; a physical demonstration of being selected by God, and at the same time, equipped and enabled by His anointing, to face any opposition; to defeat every foe; to fulfil a mission.

How significant that He chooses to do this publicly, in the presence of those who oppose you – not quietly in a corner somewhere!

I cannot help but think of the spectacle that King Ahasveros made of Haman, by crucifying him and his sons publicly on the gallows he had made for the righteous Mordechai after His deceit was exposed! (In the presence of His enemies!) Read the story in Esther 8 and 9.

In the New Testament Jesus did the same with the powers and principalities who had him crucified: "Having disarmed principalities and powers, He made a public spectacle of them, triumphing over them in it." Colossians 2:15.

This is our reward! This is our motivation! This is what keeps us going through the valleys and in the midst of trials – the Joy that lies before us! The sweetness of His presence. The comfort of His Spirit, His rod and His staff.

The Lord confirms and establishes that you are His by not only anointing your head with oil but by giving you a portion of His Spirit that cannot be contained – your cup runneth over! It is not filled to the brim, but spills over!

If you find yourself walking through deep valleys of despair at this time; if darkness surrounds you and you can see no light ... keep on walking until you reach the table He has prepared for you. Not only is He waiting for you there, but He also walks with you till you reach the end of the valley, then He sits down to dine with you.

"Weeping endures for a night, but joy com in the morning."
- Quote by King David ... a man after God's own heart.

Chapter 42

Abba

My spirit cries Abba, Father!

We are born of God.
We came out of Him.
Just as Eve came from Adam,
we were taken from Him.

"And because you are sons, God has sent forth the Spirit
of His Son into your hearts, crying out, 'Abba! Father!"
Galatians 4:6.

The Holy Spirit, Who is part of the triune Godhead, has been poured out on God's children and now lives within us. The Holy Spirit, together with our spirit, longs to be united with God the Father and God the Son.

Therefore, our spirits cry out "Abba," Father!

Our spirit longs to be united with Him. If we drift away from God, our spirit becomes 'dry.' We will constantly be unfulfilled and unsatisfied and discontent. Until the moment we are one with Him again.

Only He can satisfy the searching and yearning and longing of a believer's heart! We are bone of His bone and flesh of His flesh!

In His presence is fullness of joy and at His right hand there are pleasures forever more!

Chapter 43

I am Gomer

A Lover Who Fights for His Bride

I am blown away and broken as I read the first few books of the prophet Hosea.

God tells the prophet, a holy man, to marry a harlot and have children with her. A harlot who has many lovers.

She cannot stay away from her former lovers and runs away from him to find them whom she believes are the ones who provide her with livelihood and her luxury of grain and wine and oils.

Symbolizing the nation of Israel's harlotry and running after false gods and serving idols, God says that He will put a hedge of thorns around her, and build a wall between them so that she will not be able to find her former lovers. So great is His love for His bride, that He makes it impossible for her to find her way back to her former lovers.

Then He says, He will "allure her into the wilderness and speak tenderly to her heart." What an amazing revelation of the heart of God!

We have all played the harlot at some point in our lives. We have all been Gomer ... many times, even after we have all surrendered our lives to Christ. And instead of just letting us go and follow the lusts of our hearts and the wrong desires, He brings us into the wilderness.

And here is the most amazing thing: He brings us into the wilderness, not to punish us but to woo us back to Himself. A Lover Who fights for His bride! He's not willing to let her go!

[14] Therefore, behold, I will allure her [Israel] and bring her into the wilderness, and I will speak tenderly and to her

heart. [15] There I will give her her vineyards and make the Valley of Achor [troubling] to be for her a door of hope and expectation. And she shall sing there and respond as in the days of her youth and as at the time when she came up out of the land of Egypt. [Exodus 15:2; Joshua 7:24-26]

He allures her. In other words, He draws her to Himself; He romances her again; He lets her know she is His love. He "speaks tenderly to her heart." He whispers sweet words of love and adoration to her and assures her that He still wants her; tells her how beautiful she is. He woos her back to Himself and wins her heart once again when she realizes that it was Him Who provided the oil, the water, the grain and the wine all along. It was Him Who loved her just as she was; knowing exactly who she was, and chose her regardless!

Who can resist and withstand the wooing of such a magnificent Lover?! How can you not fall in love with Him again and again?

When she realizes Who he is, she turns her heart back to Him and calls Him, "Ishi" – my husband. My covenant Bridegroom. He will never leave me for another; He loves me, knowing who I am and what I have done, and never stops wooing me closer to Himself.

Amazing God ... how I love You, my Ishi ...

CHAPTER 44

GRATITUDE

Often times thankfulness and gratitude don't come as a 'natural' feeling but as something that has to be purposefully searched for. Looked for with focused intent, the way one would search for a lost treasure.

While it is true that there are many 'happy' seasons filled with joy and contentment, we sometimes enter seasons of difficulty, hardship and darkness.

It is easy to find joy and gratitude and laughter in seasons of abundance and overflowing provision and wonderful health – you don't even have to look for it, it's just there!

The test is to find joy and thankfulness when there is seemingly nothing to be grateful for. Then is the time when we have to seek it with purposeful intent. That is when we have to ask God to open our eyes to see the gift He gives us every day to fill our hearts with joy and gratitude! And it is there! Open your heart and your eyes and you will see it!

Chapter 45

Victory in the Midst of Suffering

According to scripture God's plan for us is to live a victorious life. This victorious life, however, might not look quite like what you think victory should look like.

Victory is not necessarily a 10-million-dollar home or a 1-million-dollar car. It is not necessarily wealth, riches, health, etc. (Although it certainly might include that!)

Victory is something that has to be achieved within yourself.

God's plan for us is clear: it is not a plan of misery. His plan for us is a good plan. A plan of welfare and peace to give us hope in the final outcome. (Jeremiah 29:11)

His plan is a plan of goodness and mercy.

I sometimes marvel at what He said in Psalm 23, namely, "Surely! (definitely!) only goodness and mercy will follow you all the days of your life." Yet, in the same Psalm, He talks about us walking through the valley of the shadow of death.

To our minds, "goodness and mercy" and "walking through the shadow of death" seem like two conflicting things that do not belong in the same sentence. Yet, God uses it like that. How does one reconcile the two thoughts?

For us, in our humanity, trials and tribulations and being in the crucible of the furnace, and drowning in many waters, do not sound like goodness and mercy!

How do you reconcile the reality that many Christians have to face sickness, poverty, unbearable pressure, loss, etc., with a gospel that teaches that nothing in your life should ever go wrong, or that as a Christian you should never experience hardship and difficulty?

Is it possible that our perspective of a victorious life could be completely wrong? Can it be that our God sometimes decides in His sovereignty that a specific person will walk a specific road which includes suffering, hardship and incredible difficulty?

We have to remember that we cannot separate God's character from His actions and decisions. His character is who He is and He cannot act outside of His character. Therefore, we cannot separate His goodness and His mercy from the trials and testing that He allows us to go through.

We have to make the mind shift and accept that His good plan for me might include a fiery furnace and severely trying circumstances. We have to learn to see His goodness and His mercy in the furnace! The furnace does not change His plan for me which is a good plan! It doesn't change the fact that He is a good God and He wants good for me!

- God's character is good!
- His nature is grace!
- His desire is to show mercy!
- That is unchangeable!

There is nothing evil or mean or spiteful about God. He is only good, therefore difficulties and hardship and pain that come our way, have to be viewed as part of His good plan for us. Our view of hardship and suffering has been distorted (as many martyrs who had the privilege to suffer for Christ will tell you!)

James cannot say it any clearer than he says it in the book of James 1, where he writes the following:

> (2) Consider it wholly joyful, my brethren, whenever you are enveloped in or encounter trials of any sort, or fall into various temptations.

In simple English, that means, "BE GLAD!" when difficulties and hardship overcome you! Celebrate, be joyful and grateful because it is part of God's good plan for you!

James further explains God's intention and the purpose of suffering in the same chapter where he says :

(3) Be assured and understand that the trial and proving of your faith bring out endurance and steadfastness and patience.

(4) But let endurance and steadfastness and patience have full play and do a thorough work so that you may be a people perfectly and fully developed [with no defects], lacking in nothing.

That is something good! That is something amazing! And that is God's plan and His purpose all along – to make you into a man or a woman, perfectly developed, lacking nothing (in your character). Those characteristics of endurance, steadfastness and patience do not lie passively within you as they grow. They are actively at work within you, changing you into a perfect man or woman, reflecting the image of Christ.

What a privilege to be chosen by God to walk a road of hardship and knowing that every difficulty, every failure, every loss, every rejection is used by Him to mould you to look more like Him!

For you to develop into a man or woman who is perfectly developed and lacks nothing, you need to go through trying circumstances and great difficulties. The characteristics of endurance, steadfastness and patience are character traits without which you will never be able to complete the purpose, mission or destiny for which God has placed you upon this earth!

- It is those who endure to the end who will be saved!
- It is those who are patient who inherit the promise!
- It is those who are steadfast and unwavering in their faith who will inherit the kingdom!

These character traits are not developed when everything is going smoothly and you face no problems or challenges. It is only when you have a problem that you cannot solve that your faith and trust in God is stretched and put to the test; it is only when you are faced with an impossibility that you call out to God to do the impossible and you need I-won't-give-up-faith and bulldog-tenacity to stand for a breakthrough!

CHAPTER 46

OUR SOURCE OF JOY

When going through pain (emotional or physical), disappointment, loss, grief, etc., one sometimes reaches a place where you lose your grip on faith completely. It is possible to actually come to a point where one has no hope for the future, no prospect of joy and fulfilment ever.

When you find yourself in the grip of depression, hopelessness and despair, it seems like an impossible feat to get back to that place of joy and peace in God.

Yet, however difficult it may seem, it is possible to get back to that place, regardless of how painful or difficult one's circumstances may be.

One of the biggest mistakes we make in life is that we try to find our joy and happiness in our circumstances – wealth, health, possessions, etc.

We have to learn that our circumstances are not our source of joy! The pleasure and happiness that wealth, health, possessions, etc., bring, are fleeting and temporary. It is not a solid foundation to build your faith upon or to be your source of joy. These are things that could change in the blink of an eye!

Regardless of how blessed we are with earthly and material things, they could and should never become our source of joy and happiness, nor our sole goal to pursue.

Of course, this in no way implies that we should not be thankful and enjoy that with which God has blessed us. It simply means that our circumstances never provide us with true satisfaction, lasting joy and total fulfilment. There is just ONE Who can provide us with that and He is the Christ!

Even in the midst of the greatest trials, hardship, and suffering it is possible to be filled with joy. Even going through the pain of failure and abandonment it is possible to feel completely loved, valued and celebrated. Even when there is no cause to be joyful in the natural it is possible to experience joy unspeakable and full of glory – in Him!

It is all found in HIM! It is only found IN HIM! He is the only true Source of joy and peace. While circumstances may change from day to day or moment to moment, He never changes. He is always there. His love never changes and His faithfulness remains the same.

When you have no hope anymore for the future; when your life has become one painful experience after the other; when disappointment and disillusionment have broken you... return to Him. Seek Him again. If you have been seeking Him, seek Him more! Follow Him harder. Press into Him deeper than ever.

He is able to restore! He can heal! He can bring fresh joy and new hope!

Let HIM be our Source of Life at all times!

CHAPTER 47

CONTENTMENT

Philippians 4:11 & 12: "Not that I am implying that I was in any personal want, for I have learnt how to be content (satisfied to the point where I am not disturbed or disquieted) in whatever state I am.

> I know how to be abased and live humbly in straitened circumstances, and I also know how to enjoy plenty and live in abundance. I have learnt in any and all circumstances the secret of facing every situation, whether well-fed or going hungry, having a sufficiency and enough to spare or going without and being in want."

The place of contentment is a wonderful place to be. It is a place of rest. It is a place of inner peace and quiet found in God. A place of complete and utter satisfaction and fulfilment regardless of your circumstances.

This place of peace and rest is found at the end of a journey of hardship and misery. A journey of lack and often going without. It is birthed in the pain of what seems to be unanswered prayers and unfulfilled promises; disappointment and hope apparently denied. It is reached after travelling through valleys of tears of hopelessness and vain attempts to gain understanding.

Then suddenly, you are there; this oasis of contentment in the desert. The waters are bitter no more but are sweet to the taste; carcasses of slain lions and bears become the treasure chest of golden nuggets and sweet, nourishing honey cakes!

That peace that is beyond understanding envelops you like a blanket and cloaks you in deep inner restfulness. Like water found in the desert a bubbling fountain of joy rises up in your spirit and you are free! Free from the shackles of fear of tomorrow! Free from the burdens of "what shall we eat and what shall we wear!" Secure in the knowledge of His love and the promise of His faithfulness, the need to know "why?" simply disappears. All fear is driven out by His perfect love.

Content simply to be in His presence, the need to ask for anything is no more and the knowledge that "He knows what we need before we even ask" becomes the reality we live by.

Wealth and possessions may give you pleasure for a while, but true lasting joy and contentment are only found in God. Circumstances, wealth or poverty, sickness or health, lack or abundance have no power to change that deep inner peace!

He prepares a table for you in the face of your enemies! A celebration, a feast in the desert! You are nourished with bread from heaven and your thirst is quenched from a stream of living waters.

Like a weaned child at his mother's breast, so I am. On my Father's lap with my head on His chest, I know that He knows and He's got it all under control. No matter what lies ahead, I have no fear and nothing will pluck me from His hand.

Regardless of the circumstances, I will remain in this place of peace. Fire and water may come; storms, wind and rain may encompass me. Yet I am at peace ... content and secure in my Father's embrace.

CHAPTER 48

THE FRAGRANCE OF CHRIST

How I long to be in Your presence Oh God! My soul longs for You as in a dry and weary land.

I cannot bear to be without His presence even for a moment. Like a needy child, I need Him and cling to Him, never wanting to let go. As a newly-wed lover, I want to be with Him every moment; to feel His nearness; to hear His voice.

Intimacy with God brings life! Intimacy with God allows you to drink from that river that flows through you. That Fountain inside of you that never runs dry.

Knowledge without life is merely that: knowledge. Simply information stored in your brain. But when that same knowledge flows from a spirit soaked in the river of God's presence it brings life. It has the power to change and transform a life!

It is not enough to know God and to know His Word – we have to dwell in His presence; we have to love His presence; to want His presence more than anything else!

Our strength comes from intimacy with God. Unspeakable joy and deep inner peace come from being with Him.

When you've been with Him, His presence lingers upon you like perfume. His glory surrounds and envelops you like a cloak. The sweet fragrance of the Rose of Sharon resting upon you brings joy and delight wherever you go.

Living in this glory sets you free from all striving. The pressure to perform and impress others disappears completely. I am solely focused on staying with Him; remaining in His presence; abiding in Him. Cloaked in His glory wisdom will flow from you. Godly counsel will come from your lips. Healing will flow to others as it flowed from Jesus; as it did when Peter's shadow fell on the sick.

In her preparation to meet with the king, Queen Esther was bathed and massaged daily with fragrant oils and herbs; her hair was infused with the smell of incense and spices until every pore in her body oozed the fragrant, perfumed oils that delighted the king.

So, it is when you spend time with the King. Your very being becomes saturated with His presence, His sweetness, His kindness. His love becomes a part of who you are. People will be drawn to you and when you leave their company, the fragrance of Christ will linger in their midst ... compelling them to seek Him again and again...

CHAPTER 49

INTIMACY

There is a place in God to which everyone is invited but few choose to go. It is found on the road less travelled and requires sacrifice, seeking, and much time spent waiting and listening. It is costly and involves death ... your death. Death to self and choosing to deliberately delight in Another. But the reward is sweeter than anything you could ever imagine.

It is a place of sweet, unbroken communion between lovers. A secret place hidden in Him where treasures are found and shared. Where unselfish adoration is expressed by a mere look, a word, a touch, a smile. A place of intimacy with my God, my Bridegroom, the Lover of my soul. A place where we meet with unveiled face as friends. Face to face with God.

David describes it so well in Psalm 27:4 where he writes:

> "One thing have I desired of the Lord, that will I seek after: that I may dwell in the house of the Lord all the days of my life, to behold the beauty of the Lord, and to enquire in His temple."

Intimacy with God is born from a deep desire to know Him. It is a natural outflow of a heart that seeks Him diligently and a passion to know who He is. In Psalm 63:1 David writes: "O God Thou art my God; early will I seek Thee: my soul thirsteth for Thee, my flesh longeth for Thee in a dry and thirsty land, where no water is; ..."

It is birthed in the desire to know and recognize His voice and to follow the counsel and guidance of the Shepherd. It is cultivated by a lifestyle of seeing His face, hearing His voice and responding.

When His presence fills me with unspeakable joy and His nearness leaves me breathless with wonder, intimacy follows naturally. When I am totally captivated by His beauty and enraptured by His splendour, I become one with Him.

In this oneness with God, I am able to hear the faintest whisper to my heart; I catch every nuance of His voice; I can see Him smile at me as we enjoy something totally insignificant to others. In this belonging to Him, I am free to be who He made me to be.

There is room for me to be dramatic, quirky, weird, eccentric ... In fact, the one thing required for an intimate relationship is honesty. Complete transparency and an acknowledgement of who I am, with all my weaknesses. And then, also, acknowledgement of who He is and what He has done for me, and more importantly, why He has done it for me.

The foundation of an intimate relationship can be nothing else than pure, unselfish love. In discovering and responding to that indescribable, undeserved, immeasurable love, a relationship of intimacy is born.

As with a new lover, it is a journey of findings of inexhaustible dimensions and immeasurable depths. A peeling away of layers and a lifting of a veil; pure delight and absolute pleasure as new discoveries are made and priceless treasures are found.

It is a journey of passion! A journey of pulsating excitement! Sometimes a journey of silent wonder and quiet fulfilment – a closeness you cannot describe...

CHAPTER 50

IN THE SECRET PLACE

Song of Solomon 2:14: [So I went with him, and when we were climbing the rocky steps up the hillside, my beloved shepherd said to me] O my dove [while you are here] in the seclusion on the clefts in the solid rock, in the sheltered and secret place of the cliff, let me see your face, let me hear your voice; for your voice is sweet, and your face is lovely."

It is not in the busyness of your day where you will meet with God; it is not when you are running from meeting to meeting and rushing to meet one deadline after the other.

Whilst He is with you wherever you go and whatever you do, it is only when you come aside in silence and solitude where you will meet with Him ... or encounter Him.

It is in the secret place that you see His face; it is there where you hear His voice, where you smell His fragrance. There where it is just the two of you, hidden in the cleft of the rock. Enclosed in an area wherein there is no space to move. Nowhere to go, nowhere to look except up... into His eyes.

It is there where He touches you with the myrrh dripping from His hands. It is in that enclosure where you smell the sweet Rose of Sharon; where He anoints you with the Balm of Gilead; where the ointment of His Name heals all your pain; puts together a broken heart. It is there where you meet with Love in its purest form.

It is only there where you experience fullness and completion; total satisfaction. Every need is met. You have encountered Wholeness.

CHAPTER 51

NAKED AND UNASHAMED

Kiss me with the kisses of Your mouth!
Let us get drunk with love
and be intimate with joyous abandon!
For our souls have fallen in love;
our flesh has become one.

Bone of my bone and flesh of my flesh.
Two hearts that beat as one;
pulsating on the rhythm of the Father's love,
forever entwined,
never to be separated again.

An arranged marriage,
through a torn veil;
consummated in a secret chamber;
a love so divine.

Guilt nailed to a tree;
shame washed away!
Face to face;
naked ... and unashamed ...

CHAPTER 52

UNDONE BY HIS LOVE

Broken and undone as my eyes are opened to see the wretched state of my heart. Overwhelmed with sorrow and grief, You choose that moment of my shame to flood me with Your love! You look right at me... through me. Your gaze undeterred by my nakedness. My eyes lock with Yours and my heart breaks at the unabashed, unashamed, all-accepting love I see in Your eyes.

My Friend... My Lord... My Love

I'm broken and undone at a love so complete; a love so undeserved! Knowing so well who I am; my weaknesses and struggles; seeing me stumble and fall time after time; yet, washing it away with incomprehensible love and inexpressible grace.

I'm broken and undone at a love so fierce it did not hesitate to say: "Thy will be done!" To save a child so wretched and poor, not aware that she was lost.

Your love melts my heart and leaves me speechless with wonder. Awash in Your grace, wrapped in Your mercy. How great is Your goodness toward me! As every new day unfolds, I discover treasures untold.

How do I comprehend a love so divine? How do I describe a love so relentless and jealous in its pursuit of winning my heart and conquering my soul?

In glorious wonder I can only cry out:

My Lord and my God! I cannot but love Thee for the rest of my days!

COUNTING IT ALL JOY

BONUS CHAPTER

Bonus

Chapter Counting it all Joy

In James 1:17-21 the Apostle James wrote: "Consider it wholly joyful my brethren, whenever you are enveloped in or encounter trials of any sort or fall into various temptations..."

What does it mean to "consider something as joyful?" It would mean to "count" it a joy or to "view" it as a joy. In the same way, one would consider it a privilege to do something for someone who cannot repay you or feel honoured to meet a very distinguished person.

In other words, the way I look at it. How do I see it? What is my perspective?

James exhorts us to look at our difficulties and hardships as a "joy." When your faith is being tried by fire, consider it all joy. A prayer not answered, think of it as a joy. A sickness not healed, financial pressure ending in bankruptcy, count it all joy. When faced with temptation and opportunity to sin, to lie, to hide something, to take something that is not yours, he says to rejoice!

How difficult is this? Are we even able to do this? Where do we find the strength of character to count something painful as joy?

Only in Him. Only when I'm connected to Him; when I'm in the Vine. When I dwell in Him constantly and remain in Him.

Only when His life-blood courses through my veins. Only when His power, His ability, His life dwells within me, I am able to manifest His character in the face of extreme disappointment, the letting go of a dream, the loss of a loved one. Only in His power am I able to deal with the fact that something I have prayed for, for years, and trusted and believed for is not going to happen.

It's only when I have lost my life completely in Him that I am able to rejoice in pain and suffering. Once He becomes my Source of life and joy as well as my Strength to endure, He also becomes my Sustenance. At that moment, when nothing else matters but to find Him in my situation and remain in Him, at that moment I am in victory and am able to "count it all joy."

In the face of the greatest disappointment, the pain of unanswered prayer, sickness that has not been healed, I am able to say: "though He slay me, yet I will trust Him!" Job 13:15.

Every day my life is poured out as a drink offering to my God. Even though I am surrounded by trouble, my heart will give thanks, and I will consider it wholly joyful!

Last Thoughts

The Miracle of the Chrysalis

The miracle inside the chrysalis... Life ... to death ... to life; the miracle of metamorphosis; the power of transformation that lies in willingly choosing to die, leaves one speechless in awe and wonder ... and total bewilderment! Could the simple caterpillar by any chance know of the beauty and splendour, the glorious freedom that awaits it when it willingly surrenders its body as a sacrifice to not only die but fall apart in the process of becoming what it was destined to be?

At the appointed time, as programmed in its DNA, it just stops eating; denying its body the food it craves necessary to stay alive. Could this low-level-no-brain cell creature know that in order to evolve, to mutate, to transform and change into a completely new being, it is necessary to deprive its cylindrical body of everything it wants, and happily embrace the process of slow but sure death?

Forming a chrysalis to keep it inside (lest the desire to escape from its destined path overtakes the creature!) it makes doubly sure that its coffin is secure and seals itself within with unbreakable silk, leaving no option to abort the plan, should it decide it no longer wants to take part in the process!

Oh! Simple caterpillar! Let me learn this from you: the joy and the freedom I long to taste is not found in this body; not in this life I live now; but in shedding the layers of this flesh one by one until all that remains is the sweet butterfly, exquisitely born from its own 'hand-spun' kist. Unwrapped from the burial cloth, it brightly comes forth with breathtaking beauty and the glorious freedom to fly!

━ ◆ ━

ABOUT THE AUTHOR

In the winter of 2015, the author, Lois Massyn van Heerden, had a life-changing encounter with God. Her life went from being an ordinary mother, raising three bouncing boys, to a passionate and radical child of God. Lois is a true lover of God and has discovered that walking intimately with God can be part of your daily, moment-to-moment life. In publishing these writings, she hopes to bring understanding to believers who have to deal with chronic pain, sickness, loss and grief, and inspire each and every ordinary Christian to push deeper and discover new dimensions in their relationship with God.

Lois has been in the ministry for 35 years and currently resides in Pretoria, South Africa. She serves the body of Christ in her calling as Prophet, Teacher, Intercessor, and Psalmist.

Read more at Lois Massyn's site.

www.ingramcontent.com/pod-product-compliance
Lightning Source LLC
Chambersburg PA
CBHW022131150726

47992CB00002B/540